Psychoanalysis, Catastrophe & Social Action

This fascinating volume uses psychoanalytic theory to explore how political subjectivity comes about within the context of global catastrophe, via the emergence of collective individuations through trans-subjectivity. Serving as a jumping-off point to address the structural linkage between collective catastrophe, subject, group, and political transformation, trans-subjectivity is the central tenet of the book, conceptualized as a psyche-social dynamic that initiates social transformation and which may be enhanced in the clinical setting.

Each chapter investigates a distinct manifestation of trans-subjectivity in relation to various real-world events as they manifest clinically in the analytic couple and within group processes. The author builds her conceptual arguments through a psyche/social reading of Kristeva's theory of significance (sublimation), Lacan's 1945 essay on collective logic, Heidegger's secular reading of the apostle Paul's Christian revolution, and Žižek, Badiou, and Jung's conception of the neighbor within a differentiated humanity. The book features clinical illustrations, an auto-ethnographic study of the emergence of an AIDS clinic, an accounting of trans-subjectivity in Black revolutionary events in the US, and an examination of some expressions of care that arose in response to the COVID-19 pandemic.

Psychoanalysis, Catastrophe & Social Action is important reading for psychoanalysts, psycho-dynamic based therapists, psychologists, group therapists, philosophers, and political activists.

Robin McCoy Brooks is a Jungian Analyst in private practice, educator and consultant in Seattle, WA. She is the Co-Editor-in-Chief of the *International Journal of Jungian Studies* and serves on the Board of Directors of the International Association for Jungian Studies. Robin is also a founding member of the New School for Analytical Psychology and active analyst member of the Inter-Regional Society of Jungian Analysts and the International Association for Analytical Psychology. Further, she is a nationally certified Trainer, Educator, and Practitioner of Group Psychotherapy, Sociometry, and Psychodrama. She currently is sheltering in place aboard a wooden boat on Salmon Bay with her husband and with two Siamese cats or their home in Bellingham, WA.

Philosophy & Psychoanalysis Book Series

Editor by Jon Mills

Philosophy & Psychoanalysis is dedicated to current developments and cutting-edge research in the philosophical sciences, phenomenology, hermeneutics, existentialism, logic, semiotics, cultural studies, social criticism, and the humanities that engage and enrich psychoanalytic thought through philosophical rigor. With the philosophical turn in psychoanalysis comes a new era of theoretical research that revisits past paradigms while invigorating new approaches to theoretical, historical, contemporary, and applied psychoanalysis. No subject or discipline is immune from psychoanalytic reflection within a philosophical context including psychology, sociology, anthropology, politics, the arts, religion, science, culture, physics, and the nature of morality. Philosophical approaches to psychoanalysis may stimulate new areas of knowledge that have conceptual and applied value beyond the consulting room reflective of greater society at large. In the spirit of pluralism, *Philosophy & Psychoanalysis* is open to any theoretical school in philosophy and psychoanalysis that offers novel, scholarly, and important insights in the way we come to understand our world.

Titles in this series:

Jung, Deleuze and the Problematic Whole
Edited by Roderick Main, Christian McMillan and David Henderson

Psychology as Ethics: Reading Jung with Kant, Nietzsche and Aristotle
Edited by Giovanni Colacicchi

Shame, Temporality and Social Change: Ominous Transitions
Edited by Ladson Hinton and Hessel Willemsen

Psychoanalysis, Catastrophe & Social Action
Edited by Robin McCoy Brooks

Psychoanalysis, Catastrophe & Social Action

Robin McCoy Brooks

Routledge
Taylor & Francis Group

LONDON AND NEW YORK

First published 2022
by Routledge
2 Park Square, Milton Park, Abingdon, Oxon OX14 4RN

and by Routledge
605 Third Avenue, New York, NY 10158

Routledge is an imprint of the Taylor & Francis Group, an informa business

© 2022 Robin McCoy Brooks

British Library Cataloguing-in-Publication Data
A catalogue record for this book is available from the British Library

Library of Congress Cataloging-in-Publication Data
A catalog record has been requested for this book

ISBN: 978-0-367-68315-3 (hbk)
ISBN: 978-0-367-68318-4 (pbk)
ISBN: 978-1-003-13687-3 (ebk)

DOI: 10.4324/9781003136873

Typeset in Times New Roman
by MPS Limited, Dehradun

Dedicated to Elliott and Ted, only love

Contents

Acknowledgments

A special thanks to Brill for granting permission to republish, Self as political possibility: subversive neighbor love and transcendental agency amidst collective blindness, first published in the *International Journal of Jungian Studies* in 2018, now Chapter One. Additional thanks to Routledge for granting permission to republish, From leper-thing to another side of care A reading of Lacan' logical collectivity, to be published in 2021 in *Shame, Temporality and Social Change* edited by Ladson Hinton and Hessel Willemsen now Chapter Two.

I am humbled by and indebted to my colleagues and friends with whom I share(d) the AIDS plague including Graham Harriman, Lusijah Marx, Lucas Harris, Wasaka Borgelt, Jessie Isaacs, Gregory Fowler, Robby Smith, Mary Kimsey, Molly Osborne, Jim O'Hearn, Dale Buchanan, Greg Carrigan, Tabor Porter, "Connie," Aaron Hornstein, Ken Ballard, Brice Winter, Deb Gruber, Shellie Barrich, Michael Mickow, Dale Buchanan, John Mosher, Romy Royce, Lusana Hubbard, Monica Spooner, Travis Penn, John Wicher and many others alive and dead. Only love.

I am grateful for the many individuals with whom I work and have worked with over the years without which there would be no book.

Ladson Hinton III opened my mind to itself through the history of ideas years ago and has graciously honored me by writing the Foreword to this book. Language does not allow me to describe my immeasurable appreciation and love.

I am indebted to Jon Mills who invited me to write a book for the Philosophy and Psychoanalysis series with Routledge and grateful for his support as he has long engaged my philosophical mind with inspirational aplomb.

Derek Hook, Lucy Huskinson and Kevin Lu's endorsements for this book gave me a booster shot of confidence that I needed for the final push to the summit while writing in and about dark times.

Michael Horne and Richard Askay sit on my shoulder.

I am grateful to the New School for Analytical Psychology and our shared vision to think into a new epoch together with anybody who wants to join us.

Many thanks to Carolyn Johnston for being a reader and Leslie Phinney for listening. Jessica Knapp was my copy editor mid-wife whose attention to detail was invaluable over the long haul.

Only love for Ted Leonhardt, my husband who contributed the art for the cover and held my heart through the thicket.

I discovered Kass Kinkead's poem inspired by Amanda Gorman in the final hour. She writes in a poem what I have attempted to write in over 70 000 words.

I am grateful to my family who inspired, challenged and accompanied me through the ordeals that background this book. They are Edna McCoy, Paul G. McCoy, Barbara McCoy, Cheryl McCoy, Paul and Anne McCoy, Barbi McCoy, Elliott P. Brooks and Amanda Barrell, Molly Long and Logan Long.

There is no book without the Routledge editor—Alexis O'Brien and the editorial assistant Alec Selwyn and others who behind the scenes deliver the book to the world. Thank you!

Foreword

Hinton Ladson

I first encountered Robin in 2004, when she was a new Candidate in the training program of *Jungian Analysts: North Pacific.*[1] I led the initial seminar, a 10-week series entitled "origins of depth psychology." It was designed as a historical and intellectual orientation to the general field of psychoanalysis. The main text was *The Discovery of the Unconscious: The History and Development of Dynamic Psychiatry.* Other major readings were by Shamdasani (2003) and Kirsch (2000). Guest psychoanalysts from other schools were invited to discuss their own traditions.

The seminar was conceived as an "immersion" experience, the goals being: (1) to develop a sense of the cultural and historical embeddedness of "depth psychology," (2) to learn about the evolution of Jungian institutes and training, including problems and conflicts. An implicit goal was to set a tone of critical inquiry and scholarship that would last through training and beyond (Hinton, 2008, p. 91).

The Ellenberger text emphasized the concept of "creative illness" as the source of the core visions of the analytic greats, along with their particular cultural and historical circumstances (Ellenberger, 1970, pp. 3–52).

This approach turned out to be traumatic to many of the Candidates. I had underestimated the degree of their idealization of Jung in particular. Seeing the truth of his "human, all too human" reality was a shock to several people.

Robin stood out quickly, manifesting her creative and scholarly mind. While being a bit shocked by the material we studied, she clearly took a vital delight in the creative freedom she gained, the space for her own ideas to emerge. I asked for written feedback after the end of the seminar, and there was 100% response! Robin's response was delightfully real (Hinton, 2008, p. 97):

> This was a masterful strategy of debunking the religion of Jung and of throwing me into a contained psychotic void from which I have...only more questions. I would entitle this stage of my training as...'Training as the death bearing stranger!' [However] ...In the course of my training...my artistic endeavors have become more prolific and I want to write more. Was that your intention by grounding us in the sacred cesspool of our historic Ganges?

This reaction highlights Robin's deeply engaged mind and soul, embracing challenge, seeing disruption as opportunity. It was the response of the creative artist too, facing the blank canvas, creating *de novo* and not simulation. This is the Robin whom I have respected as a friend and colleague for the last 16 years.

In a set of robust and scholarly creations, Robin has steadily worked out her point of view. The term "existence precedes essence," conveys this core stance. It favors process over structure, and strongly honors the *extimité* of the human condition.[2] From this standpoint, she strongly critiques "foundational" ontologies which hold the view that there is a transcendent basis for knowledge, derived from *a priori* postulates. This is a definitive theme throughout her work, including the present one.

This volume, *Psychoanalysis, Catastrophe & Social Action*, represents both a culmination and a reiteration of a profound experience of group and self during the AIDS epidemic in the 1980s, before the etiology and treatment of the disease were known. A profound experience at a retreat for the group lies at the heart of the book. Robin describes and discusses how a nocturnal episode of the sudden, uncontrolled vaginal bleeding of a participant threw everyone in the group into a vortex of caring and horror. All the attendees felt shocked, shattered, and overwhelmed, but simultaneously moved toward action and caring. This happened in ways that were both mutual and shared, as well as individual. The group experience augmented the individual experience, and vice versa, in a kind of co-individuation.

This event seems to have been a formative core of Robin's evolution as an analyst and reflective philosopher, one of those profoundly disruptive occurrences that tears gaps in self and world, and often recur throughout life, especially on the affective level. Such experiences can open creativity, their memory shaping life as they emerge and re-emerge over time, their dimensions shifting as they interact with life experience.

We thank Robin for sharing her experience and its powerful implications for self and world. It is a deep pleasure to accompany her on her moving journey of discovery, along with the rich set of philosophical and psychoanalytic companions whose perspectives she creatively engages.

Notes

1 Now called the C. G. Jung Institute of Seattle.
2 *Extimité* is a term coined by Lacan, referring to his view that what is real is just as much outside of me as inside me. Subjectivity evolves out of languaging in the broader sense, and so the Other is both strange and "at the heart of me." That is "the unconscious is outside," a creation of language (Evans, pp. 58–59).

References

Ellenberger, H. F. (1970). *The Discovery of the Unconscious: The History and Evolution of Dynamic Psychiatry*. New York: Basic Books.

Evans, D. (1996). *An Introductory Dictionary of Lacanian Psychoanalysis*. London and New York: Routledge.

Hinton, L. (2008). Teaching 'origins of depth psychology': Overview and candidate-members' experience. *Journal of Analytical Psychology*. 53, 91–100.

Kirsch, T. B. (2000). *The Jungians: A Comparative and Historical Perspective*. New York: Routledge.

Shamdasani, S. (2003). *Jung and the Making of Modern Psychology: The Dream of a Science*. Cambridge: Cambridge University Press.

Introduction: Healing is political

Approaching the psyche-politicalpsyche-political through care

(Inspired by Amanda Gorman)
May we find
In an unbroken
Stitched with love
Jazz of many voices
Each bringing their warp and weft and
Rhythm and rhyme
To a song that wasn't there before
To a future we can fall in love with.
By Kas Kinkead

It is apparent that we are living in a state of sustained emergency. The accelerating effects of global warming, the pandemic, essentialist racism, xenophobia, a widening gap between rich and poor and other atrocities leave us bewildered about what is happening or what we can do about it. Stunned by the unfathomable we may slip into the experience of massive indifference in an ever shape-shifting collective temporality of "anxious waiting."[1] Almost 20 years ago, Julia Kristeva described the modern person as one who had lost their capacity to apperceive or represent their experience in imaginatively empowered ways (Kristeva, 1995). This "malady" of the contemporary psyche, she claimed was aggravated by the uncoupling of language (thought) from the body that makes it impossible to feel

DOI: 10.4324/9781003136873-101

passionately about life in ways that one can sensibly manifest. From a different perspective, philosopher Bernard Stiegler describes the emotional and mentally fatiguing effects of chronic catastrophe as "entropic collapse" (2019, p. 8). Entropic collapse can be characterized by the inability to hold onto one's mind that leads to massive *dis*individuation, hopelessness and despair that contributes to a "loss of the feeling of existing, the loss of the possibility of expressing one's will, the correlative loss of all reason for living and the subsequent loss of reason as such, a loss [that now] strikes entire groups and entire countries" (Stiegler, 2019, pp. 8, 75–84). Indeed the existential crises at hand arose from a carelessness of thought in the first place and the withdrawal of thought from the body.

How do any of us find the courage to really break from the banality of mindlessness and open to others—to a horizon of being where we are able to remake something out of nothing for the sake of someone else in the face of its impossibility?[2] Where does this psychic momentum to "tear oneself from flesh to heart, from despondency to enthusiasm" come from (Kristeva, 1991, p. 83)? Carl Jung proclaimed in 1927 that there exists a state of mind that allows the individual to become co-effected by the shared plight of a differentiated humanity—where one may break through one's psychic fortressing thus revealing a truth of what is and the memory of thought and care in times of collective emergency. He writes from the rubble of a shattered Europe:

In this reality we are no longer differentiated persons but are conscious of our common human bonds. Here I strip off the distinctiveness of my own personality, social or otherwise, and reach down to the problems of the present day, problems which do not arise out of myself-or at least I like to imagine. Here I can no longer deny them; I feel and know myself to be one for the many, and what moves the many moves me…for here it is not the individual will that counts but the will of the species (Jung, 1927/1970, para. 261).

Jung is making an important distinction that recognizes the individuation of one is not detached from the public sphere or the concrete events of history but situated within the deep conflicts and emerging truths of the age.[3] How does this opening (reality) lead to political possibility or a culminating movement of "collective logic"—a new form of creative intelligibility and social reform within psycho-analytic practice and anywhere?

The need to care for others and to be cared for is at least partially encoded in our genes and fundamental to building what evolutionary sociologist Nicholas Christakis has described as a *good* society (Christakis, 2019). Christakis's extensive research on the biology of social behavior allows him to boldly claim that we are innately equipped as a species to band together, live cooperatively with each other, befriend each other, recognize uniqueness, show kindness, love, and reciprocity in our relationships and learn socially while teaching what we know (Christakis, 2019, pp. 135–137, 13–16).[4] Granting Christakis his hypothetical biases, his conclusions support my own regarding the ontological dimension of caring and how we may care for others beyond our own self-interests *or just as likely* remain careless. I am interested in the conditions that allow an in-dividual and/or community of people to access and optimize these innate and I add psychological (psychical) capabilities by engaging the disastrous effects of sustained even surreal catastrophic emer-gencies whose escalating pace threatens our lives daily. What allows us to surrender to the burden of being even though we are over-whelmed by the utter realness of our shared corporeal vulnerability (a universal) and psychological dependency we have on each other as little animals?[5] How does this psychical transformation occur within the individual in relation to others, society and the world? I am in-terested in how the individual is co-constituted within the very center of collective life in ways that individuate both in response to cata-strophe.[6] How is care for others awakened in the clinic and beyond? How can the psychoanalyst rebuild a sublimatory knowledge basis to creatively meet the emerging needs of our patients in our era of sustained emergency? How do we recognize our patient's political possibility or our own?

These are the central questions and concerns this book engages through a notion of trans-subjectivity. *The trans-subjective is posited as the nodal point through which the subject may move from personal concern to political responsiveness.*[7] *Trans-subjectivity is con-ceptualized as a crucial extra-psychical dimension of sublimation and a psyche-social dynamic that is the precursor to political action*—akin to what Jacques Lacan obliquely referred to as "collective logic," Julia

Kristeva as "significance," Heidegger as "having become," Gilbert Simondon as "trans-individuation" and Derek Hook, following Lacan as "trans-subjectivity" (Heidegger, 2010; Hook, 2018; Kristeva, 2000; Lacan, 2006; Simondon, 1992). My engagement with the question of the trans-subjectivity is also a critique of psychoanalysis. whose ontological and epistemological privileging of the subject disavows the socio/political dimensions of reality through which we enact our relationship to it—a problematic central to Heidegger's existential analytic of care. I submit that a psychoanalytic understanding of trans-subjectivity will allow us to expand not only how we think about psychical/social change but needs to become a part of the social reform we desire within our own discipline in the clinic and beyond.

I explore the question of trans-subjectivity from primarily two disciplines, psychoanalysis and philosophy adapting a trans-disciplinary approach. Such an approach allows me to move across different disciplines and traditions within disciplines without firmly adhering to the homogeneity of one discipline or tradition of either. The danger of this approach, of course lies in the dilution of thought through relativism without actually making a substantial objective argument. I take that risk for the sake of pushing the edges of what we already know into uncomfortable and messy off-trail possibilities so that we (those who embrace psychoanalysis) don't "burn our own house down" into the ashes of irrelevancy, as rapper Killer Mike espouses in Chapter Four.

ect" itself introduces the centrality of the psyche-social as a link between individual and society—akin to what Stephen Frosh has named, along with Gilbert Simondon half a century ago, a "psychosocial" subject that is irreducible to traditional ways that psychoanalysis, philosophy, and psychology have positioned subjectivity (Frosh, 2015, p. 1; Simondon, 1992). Instead of "psycho" (for psychology) I insert "psyche" to clarify a psychoanalytical position whose basic premise resides in understanding the psychical structures that contribute to the formation of the subject who is imbedded in a world with other beings, things, and concrete historical events. *I contend that the trans-subject is the link between the psyche-social and the political.*

The political

What do I mean by *the political*, a ubiquitous trope whose recent popularity within psychoanalytic discourse has elevated its significance to meme-like status while also invigorating possibilities for a renewed psychoanalysis.[8] To answer this question, I first turn to an introductory reading of Heidegger's existential analytic of care (*Sorge*) illuminated by Stiegler's critique (on which I lean) because for Stiegler, *care and the political are inextricably bound.*[9] Early Heidegger began to work out his notion of care through factical life experience within community life through his secular reading of Pauline doctrine that I discuss at length in Chapter One (Heidegger, 2010). *Dasein* is the term Heidegger roughly translated (from the German) meaning *existence*. Heidegger extended its use to mean existence in everyday life with others and things or "being-in-the-world "(Heidegger, 2001/1927, H 4). In later works, he would qualify the meaning of *Dasein* to denote a *possibility for* every existence in the clearing or the space between being and beings (Heidegger, 1999, p. 211). Being in this sense was dependent on the transformation of both human being and its other in the space of the clearing as Being became through its fundamental displacement and not through the single "subject" (p. 178).

The call to care (*Sorge*) is disclosed from the nothingness of the space that is the "clearing" (*Lichtung*) (2001/1927, pp. 188, 232). Being and its others were not separated from one another in the clearing and could only be apprehended (disclosed) through self-interpretation from what had heretofore been undisclosed. Care simply arrives (in the clearing) and creates a space apart from intersecting sociality with others and things.[10] Care, as such is a negative, a nothing from which Being may gain access to itself as separate from its everyday practices (p. 263). Being's authentic singularity is rendered possible against the *in*authentic being of "the they" (*das Man*) (2001/1927). In other words, there is a difference between being and human beings through which the individual must take responsibility in how to comport oneself from a mode in which human being actively opens to Being's radical alterity (Heidegger, 1999, p. 57). One must *hold sway*, in other words by bearing the hardship of the difference that arises between what is both different and intertwined in order to live out the fullness of one's life (p. 177).[11]

Stepping now into another important dimension of care...*Dasein* is also in the middle between human-being and other beings (p. 211). From the in-between or middle space *between*, *Dasein* may reach and transform both within their respective essences (p. 11). The third extrapsychical dimension of *Dasein*'s in-betweenness echoes what I delineate in Chapter Three as the trans-subjective aspect of sublimation that allows the analytic patient (or any of us) to creatively respond to something beyond one's own self-interests in a self to other engagement. This transformation occurs through human being and other beings as Being *becomes* through the enactment of both. Heidegger refers to this mysterious phenomena as *enowning* that means *bringing something into its own*. Uljana Akca eloquently elaborates enowning's enigma this way. She writes:

We cannot approach it as a rational challenge or question, but only through living it ourselves, in carrying the weight of existence as in inner polemic or strife. Dasein must become aware of its being as a matter that defines it, and yet is a fundamentally unfamiliar burden (Acka, 2017, p. 313).

I hover with Heidegger's conception of enowning because it is a basis from which we may understand how the political (a fruitful result of the "I" and "we" relation) and care (carrying the weight of existence as an inner polemic that defines ontological struggle) are inextricably bound and formulated within a psyche/social dimension. Being, in Heidegger's ontology does not have itself as its own basis and is thus fundamentally decentered and therefore cannot be seen as an isolated monad because being is constituted amidst other beings and world, as we have seen. This game-changing perspective would come into the foreground of contemporary philosophical phenomenological, structural, post-structural, and post-modern critiques eventually influencing psychoanalytic theory most notably in Lacan's revisioning of Freud's unconscious beginning mid-twentieth century.

To summarize thus far, the call of care arises with and among others but is singularly apprehended and associated with authenticity—a transient *truth* about oneself, how to live, and how to conduct oneself with others when confronted with the equiprimordiality of Being's capacity for *untruth* (Brooks, 2011, pp. 507–508). I elaborate. For

Heidegger, complete clarity or transparency can never be achieved as Being is always already hovering in-between opacity and a momentary glimpse of a transient truth about what is. *Dasein* is both what opens up and what closes off memory or rather a source of its knowledge or lack of it. Being slips back into the every-day synchrony (clock time) that reduces the past (and ways of remembering) to something "determined" through artifacts (digital archives etc.). Thus, human being neglects the poignancy of its existential character of care that is *undetermined*, thereby *slipping into carelessness* (Stiegler, 2017, pp. 393–394). Heidegger is especially concerned with how easily whole groups may regress given our equiprimordial capacity for carelessness. "The they" (*das Man*) is described by Stiegler as *dis*individuation that Heidegger, he claims *can* think into—and has to do with the falling of Being into in-authenticity, thus co-affecting a collective's *disindividuation*—an entirely psyche-social affair (Ross, 2018, p. 7).

From this background we are better prepared to appreciate how Stiegler extends Heidegger's existential analytic of care into our present catastrophic era of carelessness. Stiegler is interested in what basis Being may be open to *indeterminacy*, a dimension of mind that can be characterized by a vividness of timeless truth that allows one to imagine a livable future or other creative endeavors. Being, Stiegler proclaims is facing a new era where living toward death is no longer the crises that awakens us to a truth of what is. My reading of Stiegler on this point is that Being's contemporary challenge is more dire because the life of the entire planet (Anthropocene) is at stake not just our own lives. Therefore, it is not only the certainty of one's own death that awakens us to an *indeterminacy* that being is, but in addition we are faced with a real possibility of not having a future *at all* beyond our death due to the accelerated status of climate change (pandemics etc.) and subsequent threat of our species extinction *if we don't do something about it now*.

What moves a collective from its mindless disengagement (with the real of time's end) requires a capacity to *hold sway* or bear the burden of Being's responsibility to care about an indeterminate future for everybody else beyond one's own meager death, or beyond my own puni-verse. Daniel Ross eloquently summarizes Stiegler on the point of indeterminacy: "There is no access to the infinite of the indeterminate other than through the determinate. In short [realizing] both is what makes it possible to 'make a difference' by caring for an indeterminate future *while also* keeping in mind our tendency to close off that possibility by reducing existence to the stereotypical, the dogmatic or the careless 'common understanding' of *das Man*" (Ross, 2018, p. 4). Ross, in so many words is amplifying in contemporary language the basis of Heidegger's conception of enowning, a precondition, if you will to the question of ontological difference described above as the fundamental difference between being and beings. Stiegler thus redraws the boundaries of Heidegger's notion of care beyond its own horizon of being toward death to "being toward a life beyond my own death" while considering the real possibility of species extinction in our present era of catastrophe (Stiegler 2019, pp. 283–285).

From the basis of this sobering preparatory discussion I may now lay out what I mean by the political. Politicality as I refer to throughout is *the struggle* to *articulate* the "*I*" with the "*we*" without dissolving the "*I*" into the "*we*" (a regress to collective *disindividuation*) toward a *fruitful individuation* with an *indeterminate future*.[12] Following this line of thinking further *I posit that engaging the real (contingency) of climate change, the pandemic, xenophobia etc. opens the gap between what is failing with the subject's sociopolitical identification that generates desire for a new form of identification through which the trans-subjective may rearticulate ideological constraints leading to activism.* Thus, society may be constituted through the trans-subjective (trans-individuating in Stiegler's terms) construction of many social systems of care. *Care consists of the cultivation and transformation of trans-individuation (following Simondon) that I reconfigure through Lacan as trans-subjectivity and Kristeva's extra-psychical dimension of sublimation* elaborated in the coming chapters.

In contrast, the *careless* insurrection—encouraged by Mr. Trump, enacted by the domestic terrorists who swarmed the US Capital on January 6, 2021, in an effort to block the certification of the Electoral College vote for US Presidential Elect Jo Biden *is not* an example of fruitful activism flowing from trans-subjective authentic (consensual) truth. *The political moment, as I am using it, erupts within psyche-social sphere in-between individual and other beings mobilized by care (versus careless-ness) thus conceived as a structural dimension to human society determining our very ontological condition and possibility* (Mouffe, 1993, p. 3). In Lacanian theory, on which I lean, a *structure* concerns the *relational nature of the psyche* including its *inter- and intrarelational dimensions* mapped out through three psychical registers; the traumatic real, the imaginary and the symbolic. Catastrophe (in the material world) becomes one of the forms in which the subject encounters the traumatic real that inaugurates a call to care and political (sublimatory) possibility with and among others.

Thus far, I have identified the central question this book attempts to answer, that of the trans-subjective that I approach through a psyche/political lens. I have defined what I mean by the political that leans on philosophical and psychoanalytic references. *My objective in the following section is to orient the reader to selected thought of four luminaries for whom the psyche/social was/is of key importance (within their distinct ontologies) that backgrounds how I particularize politicality in the rest of this book. Recall, that my working thesis is that the trans-subjective is the link between the psyche-social subject and the political.* These luminaries are Jung, Lacan, Simondon, and Stiegler.

In the immediate section below entitled "Jung and Lacan," I answer the following question. Why, as a Jungian Analyst do I prioritize (to some degree) Lacan and post-Lacanian studies over Jung and post-Jungian studies engaging the question of trans-subjectivity? Following this discussion, I summarize key aspects of the groundbreaking philosophical work of Gilbert Simondon as a means of contextualizing the notion of trans-individuality from a broader field of thought while noting areas of intersection and difference in Jung, Lacan, and Stiegler.

Lastly, I engage Stiegler's concern for *thinking carefully* into a new epoch toward what he imagines will contribute to the transformation of various knowledge systems "whether this is conceptual knowledge or work-knowledge or life-knowledge" (Stiegler, 2019, p. 14). Stiegler's thought is indebted to Simondon's sweeping (yet meticulously argued) conclusion that envisions how our immediate social milieus are interconnected to an infinite number of other social, biological, technological, and psychical networks. These networks subtly and decisively influence how political, ethical, and epistemological forms of reality inform how we understand our relations between humans, nature, machines, and culture.

The final section summarizes how I have organized the chapters in this book, each deepening a certain aspect of the trans-subjective in a radicalized notion of psychoanalysis or for any of us. In the chapters that follow, I evenhandedly intersperses the rawness of clinical illustration, autoethnography, and cultural phenomena with the delicious abstraction of theory.

Psyche/social luminaries: Jung, Lacan, Simondon, and Stiegler

Jung and Lacan

Both Jung and Lacan viewed the collective realm as crucial for subject formation although each conceptualized radical alterity through very differing problematics. Both conceived of a third psychical reality through which the self or subject became constituted. For Jung, the third was the extrapsychical dimension of the psychoid archetype and for Lacan and Kristeva the third was the extrapsychical dimension of logical collectivity or sublimation, respectively. By relocating the locus of subjective identity to the real (in relation to its other interlocking imaginary and symbolic registers), Lacan and post-Lacanian theoreticians have, in my view given us a broader theoretical basis from which to understand the effects of historical, trans-historical and catastrophic trauma on the individual and its social/political milleau across time.[13] The Lacanian real (although inarticulatable—defying symbolization) contains *both* psychical and *a posteriori* (that which is known through experience) sources of trauma characterized as radical alterity. The real as radical otherness is unintelligible, inarticulatable, may not be symbolized, has no meaning, is random, experienced as pure bodily traumatisms and intangible excesses. In other words, when we encounter the *real* of a catastrophe, say the COVID-19 pandemic, our bodies and psyche's become the site for political contestation and catastrophe's claims to be worked through in psychoanalysis or elsewhere, as will be seen (Webster, 2018).

Jung's radical insight that collective psychicality was a crucial element in self-development foreshadowed later post-Lacanian thought that would extend its understanding of the subject as necessarily co-constituted with the social/political dimension of reality. However, Jung's epistemological basis for the psyche does not adequately consider how our ontological–historical–political situation defines the very basis for how we historically enact our relationship to being. As Wolfgang Giegerich claims and I am in agreement with him here—the great questions, deep conflicts, and fundamental truths of any age come out of the effects of real, concrete historical events to which we are inured (Giegerich, 2004, p. 41). Jung's originating concern for humanity's soul and its individuation became *detached from the public sphere* of the real world such as the realm of thought, politics, culture, art, science, economics, catastrophe, and so on.

Jung's focus was rather on the *private arena* of the individual's unconscious processes informed by the a-historic reservoir of the trans-personal psyche. Jung's conception of a supernatural reified collective mind fails to account for how particularity *and* universality suffuses individuality within social collectives thereby disregarding political psycho/social factors that in contrast are considered to be the very locus of subjective identity in Lacan and post Lacanian thought (Goodwyn, 2012; Lu, 2020; Mills, 2018; Saban, 2020). Otherwise put, Jung did not carefully consider the *logic* of other systems such as biology, politics, economics, culture, technology, climate crises, and world history into his configuration of the self's telos. Nor do we find in Jung a methodological means through which a self is motivated to become collectively innovative or part of social reform. However, *we must not undermine the importance of Jung's basic insight that the collective and individual are inextricably bound* even if his "un-thought out metaphysics" falls apart under the scrutiny of contemporary psychoanalytic and psychosocial discourse (Brooks, 2011; Gullatz, 2010; Hinton, 2011; Lu, 2013).

For Jung, meaning pre-existed in principle (a misconstrued transcendental idea he borrowed from Kant), was embedded in the collective unconscious and made accessible via the instincts through image and ideas (Brooks, 2011, p. 497; Jung, 1947/1954). The extrapsychical feature of Jung's later formulation of the "psychoid" factor or archetype-as-such was located in the gap between archetype (mind) and instinct (matter). Further, the psychoid was neither purely noumena (immaterial) nor phenomena (material) or jointly both. In other words, Jung was locating being, the soul and/ or self (a third unifying reality) in between mind and matter. In this sense we may say that the Jungian self, akin to the Lacanian subject is located outside of its material body and was also determined by the other. However the other that determines the Jungian self was the archetype whose meaning making possibility occurred through the extrapsychicality of the psychoid factor. While engaging radical alterity of the traumatic real is what constitutes subjectification, or rather inaugurates subject formation, in the Lacanian subject, the psychical register of the real is not composed of pre-existing universals of meaning. Recall that the real in contrast cannot be symbolized, is random, has no meaning and is experienced as pure bodily traumatisms.

Jung's disregard for the personal unconscious under and below his fascination with the objective psyche (archetypal realm) is generally known and critiqued (Brooks, 2013; Saban, 2020). Some of the basic foundationalist theoretical assumptions that shaped Jung's clinical work were contained within a thesis of historical immanentism founded upon an overarching meta-narrative that posited all things within a necessary unity, out of which the "self" archetype emerged whose comprehension compelled one toward a telos of wholeness (McGrath, 2012). When a so called archetype emerged, Jung retained a stance of epistemological authority when it came to archetypal explications regarding the patient's experience (Brooks, 2013; Jung, 1935, para. 190). At the level of the personality or personal unconscious, however Jung's method dramatically shifted. At the personal realm he conceived a differentiated humanity and addressed the patient as an individual irreducible to others including himself. He writes: "I talk with them as one natural human being to another, and I expose myself completely and react with no restrictment" (Jung, 1935, paras. 318–319, 174). Jung's phenomenological/descriptive approach was a method he developed and retained from his earlier and acclaimed word association test research conducted at *Burghölzli* Psychiatric Hospital in Zurich in 1901–1904 that I personally model my own practice after (Bair, 2003, p. 66). In this approach, Jung would enter a discursive back and forth process between analyst and patient that followed the patient's associations to their own material that he would amplify thus opening what may lead to a sublimatory dimension of analysis. We are less bound to interpretive dogma using Jung's phenomenological/descriptive approach when engaging enigmatic material and free to be shaped by an ensuing process that emerges in between self and other as I discuss in Chapter Three.

I have come to think of archetypes as provisional universals producing both singular and cultural particularities that may be shared. When these provisional shared realities are recognized they may become a basis for consensual reality opening political possibility for individuating a collective or may alternatively disindividuate a collective into carelessness. I will first give you an example of consensual reality whose organizing outcome is destructive, careless and disindividuating. The aim of the fantasy construction of white superiority generated through white discourse (over centuries) was/is to maintain the hegemony of white superiority by projecting what *I lack* onto the racial other (who reifies my lack) and has a traumatic effect on African American's sense of being today (George, 2016, p. 31). As I discuss at greater length in Chapter Four, white fantasy objects of race establish whiteness as a hierarchical status by casting other races into *non-being*, what Lacan would call the master signifier of what determines being (Ibid). The fantasy object of *other race as non-being* and *white race as superior being* gestures toward a more contemporary application of an "archetype" but would need to shed Jung's epistemological basis to consider such a revisioning viable. Such an application can be observed in how collectives may organize themselves around a shared signifier (symbol) when encountering a catastrophe. An example I describe in Chapters One and Two is how the real of HIV positive blood became a master signifier of concern and horror that mobilized an entire group into consensual caring and life-saving action. This trans-subjective moment is depicted on the cover illustration *in contrast to* the subjugating master-signifier of race (as non-being) that fantasy constructions of white superiority perpetuate across the globe.

These provisional universals include both psychic and/or experientially based phenomena that are inextricably bound yet distinct and may flash up when encountering the shared traumas of our era. *In trans-subjective moments, the subject can begin to translate particularity into some kind of universality, one that levels distinctions between others by recognizing what is common among ourselves as peoples over time but, at the same time does not disallow what remains irreparably separate* (Brooks, 2016). Think of Christakis's partially genetically encoded sensibilities that allow our species to collaborate and care about each other in group life, *or not*. Think of Butler's claim that we are joined (as a species) by the biological *and* psychological vulnerability of our bodies. The truth of this claim, while seeming obvious remains enigmatically out of reach unless we are brought to our knees by a soul shattering crisis.

Heidegger has warned us, however that we are just as vulnerable as beings to slip out of the memory of caring into crowd mind or entropic collapse. Let me give you another example of what I mean by universals that colonize versus particularize a shared truth such as our biological and psychological precarity revealed to us during the recent pandemic. A maddening and ubiquitous meme we see blasted on social media and in public spaces is; *We are all in this together*. While the virus does not discriminate who it infects (a universal), some individuals live in conditions that render infection more likely (crowded structures, homelessness, living with children, front line health/care staff with or without adequate PPE, and other essential workers). Still, others are more vulnerable to its deadly outcomes (pre-conditions known and unknown, age, race, etc.), and still others have better access to healthcare where early detection and treatment may save a life or minimize how the virus ravages the body. Memes such as this are totalizing structures that reify particularities into a universal that tacitly colonizes distinctions into propagandizing presuppositions—a violent Hallmark card.

For Lacan, the world takes hold of the subject through its radical encounters with catastrophe thus opening what is obscured on the symbolic/political dimension of reality. In Chapters Two and Four, I conduct a close and particularized study of Lacan's 1945 essay elaborating the structural movements between subject, intersubjective and trans-subjective logic culminating in an expression of a shared solution to a dilemma posed by the traumatizing real of AIDS and George Floyd's killing respectively (Lacan, 2006). Lacan's three registers of psychical reality, in my opinion provide a broader platform through which we may better theorize the effects of catastrophe on the visceral (the real of natural phenomena), the subjective (intersubjective imaginal fantasy level), and sociopolitical dimensions of experience (symbolic realm) in the modern world and consider how these experiences may contribute to political agency.

Lacan regarded Jung's epistemological basis for the collective un-conscious as too narrowly confined and rooted in the imaginary order, only one of (his) three realms (Gullatz, 2010, pp. 691–698; Lacan, 1988, pp. 114–117; Lacan, 2006, p. 195). From this pro-spective a central problem in Jung's ontology (according to Lacan) was in falsely situating the truth of the self/subject at the level of imaginary semblances (archetypal image or idea) instead of the al-terity of the Other of the socio/Symbolic realm whose singular truth is revealed in the subject's encounter with the real. Gullatz elaborates this point below:

Archetypal theories are rooted in some genuine intuition, in the depths of one's experience of the imaginary order....the infinite re-gress of imaginary symmetries does not finally come to a halt in the Real of natural phenomenon—the archetypes wherein an imaginary fragment that has been placed into the inner "hall of mirrors" would be anchored. The regress of imaginary semblances can never come to a halt in so far as it remains caught up in its own circuit, unmoored from any direct connection to the Real" (Gullatz, 2010, p. 692).

The archetypes Gullatz is referring to are anchored in an inner hall of self-referencing mirrors in the individual's mind without any direct connection to real concrete events within the public sphere. Singular truth for the Jungian subject arises in its encountering archetypal material that in and of themselves are only emissarial messages (pre-determined meaning) delivered from the world soul.[14] One has the impression that the Jungian self is being crafted as Matryoshka nesting dolls whose many pieces of decreasing size placed one inside the other point only to itself as an undifferentiated solipsistic totality having self/God as its own basis. Such a self-referential holism ne-gates and/or subsumes all non-archetypal, non-psychic, particular-ized and *a posteriori* (experience based) aspects of the mind into a diffuse totality guaranteeing a homogeneous immanent discourse residing within it-self.

On the other hand, Jung's engagement with the Apostle Paul, Nietzsche's *Zarathustra,* and his conceptions of kinship libido and enantiodromia became indispensable in my formative investigations of self as political possibility as will be seen in Chapter One.

I now turn to an overview of Simondon's ground-breaking philo-sophical opus that emerged in the middle of the twentieth century

France. Simondon's collected works have in recent decades re-vitalized intellectual interest including Jungian scholars such as Saban and Chabot who see in Simondon a (trickster-like) basis from which we might creatively revision aspects of Jung's ontology (Chabot, 2003; Saban, 2020).[15] My interest in Simondon is directed specifically to highlighting how he originally formulated a notion of trans-individuation and how I may carry the bare bones of his thesis forward into a psychoanalytic perspective so that we may revitalize the clinic, our institutes, and our organizations in the pervasive shadow of catastrophe. However, Simondon's notion of transindi-viduation is only a pearl on a string of a much larger imaginary that requires contextual elaboration especially if we are to grasp the sig-nificance of Simondon's thought in how Stiegler carries it forward and building on Stiegler how I attempt to revision the political into psychoanalytic theory and practice.

Gilbert Simondon's radical notion of psyche/social individuation

Simondon was alarmed that the boundaries demarking our relation between machines and humans, nature and human, nature and technology were not carefully considered within academia (Simondon, 2015/1965, p. 506). Thus, his theory of individuation was also a critique of the human sciences whose ontological and episte-mological privileging of the subject, he claimed disavowed the pro-blem of the individuation of the group—a critique you are by now aware I share.[16] One of the primary benefits of Simondon's theorizing ontogenesis as a basis for psychic and collective individuation is that it provides a speculative perspective that brings together sociological, psychical, biological, and technological realities without reducing one into the other (Scott, 2014). The problem of individuation, for Simondon began not with the individual (or psychical being) but with individuation itself—whose very outcome was iterative, in-determinate, and open ended in relation to its world. Individuated self-knowledge therefore shifts any ontological assumptions from "the becoming of individuated being" to "the becoming of the in-dividuation of being" (Scott, 2014, pp. 5, 20–21).[17] Knowledge of oneself, in other words is acquired via a *process of becoming* in re-lation to its milieu and its operations are *performative, lived, enacted*

among and with others and things and so on. From this basis
Simondon could posit that *the ontogenesis of being is internally generated from the processes of individuation itself.* From this perspective,
there is no universality of knowledge from which the individual
comes to know itself or can be known including what those conditions for knowledge are.

We can see that Simondon would be opposed to Jung's unitary
reality of the collected unconscious. Indeed, Simondon's approach to
individuation radically challenges the foundationalism woven into
analytical psychology, especially the presuppositions that include the
validity of a set of *a priori* cognitions viewed through the lens of an
isolated mind with its innate structures and conventions of interpretation that privilege the illusion of the analyst's epistemological
authority, and the universality and essentialisms fundamental to
Jung's rendering of the self (Brooks, 2011, p. 498). While Simondon
was influenced by Jung's elaborations on psychical individuation
(including his alchemical allegory of individuation) and expanded
notion of libido (in contrast to Freud), his project ventured much
further into multiple co-affective modalities of individuation through
which new kinds of sociality and collectivity could be imagined
(Chabot, 2003, pp. 109–126; Scott, 2014, p. 73). His imaginary sought
to think of natural (science), psychical (being), collective, and me-
chanical (technics) processes as involved in *any* and *all* constructions
of individuation (Simondon, 1989).[18]

Both Lacan and Simondon engaged structuralism's imperative to
decenter the subject from its unitary, transcendental autonomous
agency that can master the world through its reason. Therefore,
Simondon's psychical individual and the Lacanian subject were entirely dependent on its inter-relationship to a social dimension for
subject formation echoing aspects of Heidegger's investigations into
the ontological dimension of human being that showed up in in the
stream of everyday life in the phenomena of everyday social contexts.
Simondon rigorously argued that human evolution owes its existence
to a connection between technology and society and challenged us to
become "intuitive" technicians of the human species by refocusing
our inventive potential in a co-evolution with biology, technical
systems, and culture (Simondon, 1989, 2012/1958, p. 224).[19] I often
think of Simondon's emphasis on the importance of *mindful*

partnering with technology through our growing dependency on ZOOM and other technological platforms that allow us to safely isolate while staying in touch in cyberspaces with friends and family and business contacts during the pandemic.

In order to explicate the genesis of human individuality co-effected by other individuating systems further, it was necessary for Simondon to formulate a system of reality he called the "pre-individual." The pre-individual was the first phase of being (psychical) and as such remained an inexhaustible resource of generative possibilities and diversifications in its relationship with the world based on senses, emotion, and language. The system of the pre-individual did not presuppose either psychic or social register but consisted of a system that was constituted by the individuation (evolution) of the living being itself. Psychic individuation was a social process whereby the living being reached beyond itself leading itself toward others in a wider system of the world, then folded back into itself in order to amplify the processes of differentiation repeatedly through life (Simondon, 1992, p. 307).

Simondon denoted two types of individuation in relationship with others through which singularity and belonging are at stake. The first mode of individuation was personal and involved maintaining the status quo with others guided by what one needed to belong by acquiring a stable network of shared experiences based on shared ideologies and ways of being. The future imaginary of the individual was thus contained by social memory of the past and summoned forward by cultural expectations of what is valued and possible through the lens of a particular social milieu. Personal individuation was engaged through communication with others via the structures of language and social norms, but these very social norms prohibited novel expression. Simondon's personal mode of individuation has parallels to Lacan's Symbolic realm characterized by codified systems of rules, laws, social practices, and ideologies that give us identity but also restrict creativity. We can see the structural conflict Simondon was establishing between the boundless creative possibilities contained within the strivings of the pre-individual against the restrictive forces of normativity required for social belonging that become the fertile ground from which political possibility (my terms) could arise for both Lacan and Simondon but from a different problematic.

Simondon identified the second tier of psychical individuation as "transindividuality" that was crucial for the possibility of collective individuation (Scott, 2014, p. 76). What precipitates the individual's movement toward transindividuality and the coalescing of individual and collective individuations into a novel form of sociality? Simondon postulated that the fundamental restrictive norming pressures that limit authenticity summoned the desire for being in more socially compatible situations and for finding a resolution. The questioning of being's authenticity (in Heideggarian terms), in other words summons being back to its pre-individuality, the primal source of authenticity, limitless possibility and to new forms of individual and collective knowledge (Simondon, 1992, p. 310). For Simondon, the "seat of [self]-knowledge" ... was the "true process of in-dividuation" and through its iterative processes the individual was better suited to think for itself amidst others (Simondon, 1992, p. 309). The transindividual, therefore was called to co-create a new social reality and was challenged to generate new forms of knowledge through a vigorous interactive exchange between "that which is larger than the individual and that which is smaller" (or the pre-individual) (Simondon, 1992, p. 310).

Relatedness through the pre-individual was always singular, and for Simondon always occurred within the context of a collective. The transindividual is the product of a new individuation that requires a more profound engagement with itself into its affective resources (via the pre-individual). This process allows the transindividual to be able to adopt a new attitude and openness with the *other as other*. The trans-individual therefore has a capacity to engage a differentiated humanity akin to what Kristeva would refer to as an "impossible unity of strangers" (Kristeva, 1991, p. 77). But how does the opening lead to an openness of one to another? For Simondon, *transindividuality of one allows for other individuals to communicate at the level of the pre-individual,* thus making it possible for entry into new collective in-dividuations (Simondon, 1992, pp. 307, 310–311). From this basis we may better understand Simondon's claim that the phenomenon of collective individuation is the *true psychosocial* from which the *trans-individual* arises (Simondon, 1992, pp. 248, 302). This transindividu-ating "we" holds powerful resonances with how I build my case for the trans-subjective leaning on Lacan and Hook in Chapters Two, Three, and Four (Hook, 2018). *Lacan's notion of collective logic—the vector of transforming consensuality in the face of a shared trauma—has certain resonances with Simondon's notion of transindividuality particularly the supposition that the human subject is both constituting and being constituted by the objective (not in the Jungian sense) and not the psychical realm alone.*

For Simondon, Stiegler, Lacan, and Jung (within distinct ontologies) subject formation is performative requiring multiple self/other meditative (folding back into itself) engagements as it moves toward what it cares about or is concerned about in order to have meaning giving context of its world. You will recall that Saban sees present in Jung's collective unconscious a potential that is yet "unthematized" that can be revisioned in the form of Simondon's pre-individual (2020, p. 96). This would require, Saban furthers a "creative reengagement with the psycho-social… "where individuality is not only a product of psychic individuation but directed toward the collective," and I add multiple co-affective both material and immaterial processes of individuation that Simondon elaborates in his works (Saban, 2020, pp. 96–97). As already discussed in the last section, the incompatibilities between Lacan and Jung's problematics remain a relevant consideration when imagining how one might theoretically liberate the Jungian self from its foundationalist entrapments into the multifaceted co-effected public sphere—a door Simondon has opened that Lacan, Stiegler and others have walked though. Can we envision a post-Jungian version of Simondon's trans-individual, a nodal point through which the subject co-effects its social world *from within* Jung's ontology that exceeds and/or engages the cultural/mythological considerations Jung hung his hat on in such a manner that does not reify, essentialize, or colonize difference? Or can we simply move on and take what of Jung's thought remains relevant in today's crises of civility and rethink it within broader perspectives, thereby not throwing his whole corpus under the preverbal bus? Clearly, I favor the latter position.

From this overview of Simondon's contribution to the history of ideas, we are better prepared to grasp Stiegler's theoretical indebtedness, and mine thorough him.

Bernard Stiegler's plea for thinking the impossible

I turn to Stiegler's imaginary as a way into the discussion of what we can actually do about massive entropy on any level of social engagement and how this might be relevant to those of us reading this book. Stiegler especially uses Simondon's conception of *transindividuation* as a theoretical point of departure for his vision of an alternative way of life in our present era of catastrophe whose very basis requires a *return to self-reflection as a collective practice.*[20] Simondon's conceptualization of multiple, distinct, and ontogenetically generated individuation processes allowed Stiegler to extend and amplify the uncritically held destructive effects of technological individuation on the other individuations. The unmediated effects of uncritically held technological developments accompanying the digital age that contribute to "vertiginous increase in entropy" are explicitly developed in Stiegler's text *Automatic Society, Volume I: The Future of Work* (2016). Here, Stiegler expansively describes another form of generalized entropy in relation to our present historical juncture mediated by Anthroposcenic despair:

> under what conditions is [it] still possible to *think* in today's era of the Anthropocene, in which the human has become the key factor in the evolution of the biosphere, considering the fact, structurally neglected by philosophy, that thinking is thoroughly conditioned by a technical milieu...The Anthropocene results from modern technology's domination of the earth through industrialization that is currently unfolding as a process of generalized, digital automation which tends to eliminate reflection and to block any genuine questioning of its own development, producing a state of generalized entropy at all levels – ecological, psychic, social, economic, and, in particular, the noetic or thinking. (p. 386)

Stiegler is concerned with thinking's *disindividuation*, another concept he borrows from Simondon, that means what it sounds like—a moving away from the conditions of individuation at any tier and particularly our ability to think critically into the feeling of the world's wound that presents itself—such as the terrifying effects of catastrophe. While he references the works of Freud intermittently and Winnicott (2013) he only occasionally references Lacan. The Lacanian analyst encourages the patient to turn toward the real of the personal psychical wound (*après-coup* event) that enables the patient to more adeptly engage the ferocity of the body's affective drive tensions that animates the subject's movement toward a sublimatory process. Stiegler, perhaps inadvertently extends a Lacanian conception of *après-coup* (immediate trauma of any kind that reveals traces of a primal wound) to world catastrophe thus opening the door to the ways in which catastrophe may awaken a call to care. In order to invigorate sublimatory thought (to make a difference) Stiegler claims we must hold onto our minds first and secondly think with others beyond the ideological frames of yesteryear whose major premises do not apply to our present era.

According to Stiegler, Simondon *can think* the dynamics of a relation of the "*I*" to the "*we*," but he fails to consider the *they* in relation to "*I*" and "*we*." Simondon, he claims *cannot* think into or break down the human experience of collective "disindividuation" or the massive *loss* of individuation for the individual and its collective "leveling down of all possibilities of being" in relation to advancing technology that is manipulated by the invisible hand of hyper-globalized neoliberal agendas that we find ourselves in now (Stiegler, 2019, p. 29). Recall Stiegler's observation that Heidegger *can* think the regress to collective disindividuation ("the they") but his philosophical imaginal cannot grasp the possibility of a "genuinely fruitful collective individuation process (a "we") other than the dissolution of the "I" into a "we" equated by the "*Volk*"—the tragic effects of nationalism (Ross, 2018, p. 7). Ultimately, Stiegler is concerned with conceptualizing how we may carry the weight of our existence as an inner polemic that defines our ontological struggle as it applies to whole systems. That is, our *becoming as a society* is an enactment of both (enowning) to individuate (caring) *and* disindividuate (carelessness) thus revisioning both Simondon and Heidegger's distinct contributions to a larger vision of saving the world and ourselves from our disindividuating tendencies.

Stiegler is interested in collective dis-individuation's homeopathic remedy or that of creative innovation (sublimation's possibility) that may contribute to a society's transformation. The wound's reality, according to Stiegler (echoing early Heidegger) is received through the senses (affect) and evokes a kind of demand or calling to do what is necessary (Stiegler, 2018, p. 399). Put another way, thinking into the question of the Anthropocene, is akin to encountering the Lacanian real (not a connection I am aware Stiegler made) through its contingent, traumatic effects whose very definition lies in its utter resistance to symbolization and is therefore inarticulatable, unintelligible, and incomprehensible. Such a traumatic engagement with the real opens up spaces for the ethics of singularity by paradoxically driving the subject's relation to others arousing a call to care (Brooks, 2016). Stiegler further elaborates what he means by the mechanism through which we may save ourselves via the transindividual construction of many social systems.

Yet, if we take Simondon seriously, when he states that the psychic individual (the *I*) can individuate itself effectively only by participating in collective individuating (the *we*), then it is indeed necessary for there to be collective individuation, which can constitute itself only by distinguishing itself from other collective individuations, that is, through this collective identification that a *we* forms (2019, p. 31).

In this way, a catastrophic event becomes the meeting place between the individual and society where the trans-subjective possibility may arise. *In this sense, we can posit the trans-subjective is the link between the psyche-social and the political possibility.* If one accepts the call from the wound of a dying world and the incumbent crisis of civility, eventually, society can be constituted through the *transindividual* construction of *many* social systems of care into a new epoch.

Stiegler does not stop here. His project is to think into the possibility of a *new epoch* that on the global level liberates the individual from its symbolic misery into sensibility or the ability to relate to the world with others ("we") through a renewed sensible aesthetic. Such an epoch is not where he situates us now. We have since drifted past the tipping point where Anthroposcenic denial advances us toward our own extinction. Stiegler places us in the precarious gap between the Anthroposcenic era philosophically gesturing toward a new age that remaps agency, power and thought that he names the Neganthropocene (2018).[21] Such an aesthetic, he argues is crucial so that individuation (in all of its forms) may occur through all dimensions of noesis (Stiegler, 2019, pp. 227–228). What comprises noesis or rather a noetic life through which a new normative knowledge is engaged? On this Stiegler writes:

> a vital knowledge of milieus, systems and processes of individuation – where knowledge is the future of life. Here the concrescence of the cosmos generates processes of individuation in which entropic and negentropic tendencies play our differently in each case. (2018, p. 41)

Here Stiegler carries us into the very center of Heidegger's ontological divide and urges us bear the tensions that threaten to divide us, lull us to return to the (death driven) somatic realm of the mother's body or throw our being toward impossible possibility, the indeterminate negentropic dimension. *Thinking because our lives and the fate of the planet depends on it* is the answer Stiegler concludes at the end of his life—in a sweeping somewhat autobiographical text he entitles *The Age of Disruption* (2019). Stiegler's plea, presented here in the broadest of brush strokes calls on each of us to turn toward the singular wound of our existence that presents itself in our present crisis of civility and become activated by it, to think into it with others toward new subversive expressions. These radicalizing perspectives will contribute to, he poignantly writes:

> the emergence of new forms of thinking is translated into religious, spiritual, artistic, scientific, and political movements, manners and styles, new institutions and new social organizations, changes in education, in law, in forms of power, and, of course, changes in the very foundation of knowledge – whether this is conceptual knowledge or work-knowledge or life-knowledge. (2019, p. 14)

Let us catch our breath from the magnitude of this statement. I am most moved by Stiegler's optimism for the healing potential of collective life that does not separate thought from the reals of contemporary existence and secondly envisions how each of us within our spheres of influence may contribute to changing the "very foundation of knowledge."

I first became aware of what I am now calling the trans-subjective dimension of group life when I was a young therapist co-leading group experiences with individuals who were living with AIDS in Portland, Oregon. These experiences radically challenged what I thought I knew about how to think or practice psychotherapy or the ways in which care can be collectively expressed among a differentiated humanity. In 2017, I began to research the question of the healing power of collective life and this book is my meditation. While the bones of trans-individuation are found in Simondon and Stiegler' philosophical treatises, they do not thematize how these processes show up in clinical practice including within group dynamics, nor should they. Both have rigorously philosophized a notion of trans-individuation from their distinct problematics breaking the trail for any of us to amend for our own purposes. My objective, as stated above is to subversively think into a notion of trans-subjectivity born from my own clinical experience and from the vicerality of my little animal body living in our era of sustained emergency. The best of what I have written comes from the space between the vicerality of the work and the abstraction of thought through it.

Lacan does not go far enough conceptualizing the trans-subjective moment in collective life even though much of his narrative foreshadows later political theorizing by Žižek (2015), Hook (2018), McGowan (2016), Badiou (2003), and Stavrakakis (1999) to name a few. Jung envisions the problem, but his ontology lacks a persuasive psyche/social perspective grounded in the public sphere of the real world. Kristeva is reluctant to extend her exquisite rearticulation of sublimation outside of a traditional clinical realm. My sublimatory call to care in response to the reals of our world flows, drips, dribbles, and blazes a path in the following pages.

Synopsis of chapters

The chapters are chronologically arranged in the order they were written. The first chapter is entitled "Self as political possibility: subversive neighbor love and transcendental agency amidst collective blindness" and was completed in 2018. This essay provides the reader with an expansive backdrop to my thinking that I particularize in later chapters. I investigate a notion of self as political possibility from a multi-disciplinary perspective engaging the psychoanalytic thought of Jung, Žižek, Badiou, and Heidegger.

I illuminate my theoretical arguments with an auto-ethnographic study of the conditions from which an egalitarian-based clinic of care emerged amidst the horror of the AIDS plague when there was no societal support in place. The process of conducting an ethnographic study unearthed my visceral memory of AIDS and the transforming moments our community came together in powerful surges of agency, provoking new waves of mourning and indebtedness. In Chapter One, I begin my investigation into how we can understand the conditions that allow for emancipatory revolution of groups that have collective individuating consequences. Lastly, I engage Heidegger's (and Jung and Badiou's) secular reading of the apostle Paul's Christian revolution as a means of elaborating the extrapsychical dimension of thought and the conditions for its collective and co-experienced political possibility in today's catastrophic era.

The second chapter is entitled "From leper-thing to another side of care: a reading of Lacan's logical collectivity" completed at the onset of COVID-19 in 2020. The essay is entirely developed around a singular clinical moment that arose within a therapy retreat with persons living with AIDS highlighted in Chapter One. The terrifying and tender scene of Bonnie's bleeding out haunted me, and I was inspired to more deeply engage what happened there from another frame of reference. Working with the underlying psychical dynamics of the scene, I elaborate a notion of trans-subjectivity through a close reading of Lacan's 1945 essay entitled "Logical Time and the Assertion of Anticipated Certainty." Lacan delineates three iterative moments of time that culminate in a profound expression of collective truth. Depicted are the psychical structures underlying the movements between the subject engaging the visceral real of Bonnie's blood and what that foretold through an intersubjective search for identity (Who am I and what does she want of me?) and the culminating expression of a shared solution to a dilemma posed (taking collective responsibility). The times were dark and illuminating. Solidarity existed in those trans-subjective moments that lifted and informed individuals and sometimes groups of individuals toward a kind of concrete action that often furthered its own ethically driven purpose.

I locate my study of the trans-subjective in the clinical realm of the office in Chapter Three. The chapter is entitled "A subversive reading of Kristeva and sublimation." This essay was completed in 2020. Julia Kristeva is a post-Lacanian psychoanalyst and theoretician whose prolific publications carry her distinct psychoanalytic contributions into cultural studies. Through a close reading of Kristeva's sub-limatory notion of "significance" I identify, critique and clinically il-lustrate the extrapsychical dimension of trans-subjectivity. For Kristeva, psychoanalysis enables the patient to more adeptly engage the ferocity of the body's affective semiotic forces (mobilized by drive, desire, and *jouissance*) that animates the subject's movement toward the Symbolic realm in a sublimatory process of significance. Kristeva's theoretical debt to Lacan is also discussed as well as the differences within their thought. Sublimation, and particularly the third dimension of trans-subjectivity can be seen as the lynch pin for all creative iterative productions that not only contribute to the subject's com-plexity/maturity but also contributes to a co-individuating force within the transference in the analytic scene and outside of the office. Whereas Kristeva is reluctant to extend psychoanalytic theory/practice into the political realm, I elaborate a broader vision of what can account for a psychoanalytic conception of sublimation in an era of sustained cat-astrophe. I illustrate the development of my thesis with many case illustrations throughout the essay.

The final chapter is entitled "Trans-subjective agency illustrated in the reals of US (post) slavery racisms." I ambitiously link the notion of trans-subjectivity to a socio/political scale through a study of US black revolutionary organized in three parts. The first part conducts a socio/historic overview of black revolutionary struggles that maintain and challenge the remediation of racial ascription today. From this background, I elaborate a notion of political time in the (post) Civil Rights era through its various collective atemporal indexes. The psychosocial and anthropological studies of (post) apartheid South Africa conducted by Derek Hook and Vincent Crapanzano respec-tively are referenced. Lastly, through a reading of Lacan's 1945 essay entitled "Logical Time and the Assertion of Anticipated Certainty" I explore how we may articulate the subject's movement through three yet interlocking temporal psychical processes culminating in trans-subjectivity. I situate the notion of trans-subjectivity within Michael

Santiago Render's (stage name Killer Mike) speech delivered on May 29, 2020 following the tragedy of George Floyd's killing. Listening to and transcribing Render's speech became a sublimatory call to caring for me and I began to write this chapter that weekend. I reference the works of Frantz Fanon and Lacanian scholar Sheldon George whose insights into what accounts for African American agency. The symbolic instantiations of race are considered.

Notes

1 I discuss at length various modes of collective temporality in Chapter Four with regard to the present moment of the civil rights movement within a historical trajectory. The term "anxious waiting" is borrowed from anthropologist C. Crapanzano who in his text *Waiting The Whites of South Africa* (1952) describes indexes of political temporality within apartheid South African society.

2 I discuss the significance of this statement in Chapter Two through a reading of Julia Kristeva's notion of sublimation. In describing sublimation's dynamics she states: "...I am able to remake nothingness, better than it was and within an unchanging harmony here and now and forever, for the sake of someone else. Artifice, as sublime meaning for an on behalf of the underlying, implicit non-being, replaces the ephemera...Sublimation alone withstands death (1987, pp. 99–100).

3 Jung's keen observation contradicts his general disregard of the public sphere versus the private arena of the individual's unconscious processes informed by a trans-personal psyche. I discuss this tendency in the Jung and Lacan section below. Jung's thought is wrought with contradictions, irregularities, and confusing trajectories as has been well discussed in the literature and frankly not unusual if we follow the thought of any great mind (Heidegger, Lacan) over decades of prolific dedication to a theory of mind.

4 Within months of Christakis's text *Blueprint: The evolutionary Origins of a Good Society* 2019) was published another text taking a position on the matter of what makes us human was published by Robert Plomin entitled *Blueprint: DNA Makes Us Who We Are.* (2019). Both are well researched and argued with critiques from different sides of the nature (genetic determinism) vs. nurture (culture) debate. Science is a conversation that reaches to the edge of what we know through data and hypotheses that follows data in a way that is the least biased (conversation with Elliott P. Brooks, June 2020). Here, I acknowledge that my confirmation biases falls on the side of overreaching optimism regarding what is possible within the human revolutionary spirit to transindividuate in the face of its own destruction.

5 Judith Butler is most interested in creating a human ontology that invigorates radical social transformation with an agenda of *inclusivity.* Her ontology of human life requires we recognize *our shared corporeal vulnerability* and

interrelationality *as a basis for making political responsiveness possible.* We are given "over to others" from the beginning of our lives, she claims by virtue of the social/political/cultural vulnerability of our bodies. These vulnerabilities are made known to us through the fact of psychological and biological dependencies we have on each other, the risk of losing those attachments and subsequent risk of psychological and/or physical violence because of this exposure (Butler, 2006, pp. 19–49). Thus, bodily being is mailable to social and politically articulated forces inscribed into our collective ideologies, biases and actions that have already been developed historically and determine what a human life is or is not. During the COVID-19 pandemic, for example, we are tragically exposed to socio/political mandates that determine whose life is worth saving (medical rationing), whose suffering is recognized, mourned, and resourced and lastly whose life may continue to flourish or be allowed to imagine into a future worth living?

6 By individuation I am referring how we increase complexity as beings through how we engage various realities over time within a sort of co-evolution of psyche, biology, technology, society, and so on. I am in alignment with Gilbert Simondon's thesis that I engage below.

7 I have put in italics throughout what I consider to be a working purposeful theoretical summary of underlying arguments central to this book.

8 Certainly Andrew Samuels is a giant of ground-breaking thought regarding politics and psychoanalysis in Jungian studies (Samuels, 2001, 1993, to cite a few). He identifies many issues, dangers and possibilities in his many books generously opening the door for others to join him or extend some of his central ideas across psychoanalytic disciplines. See also Kiehl, Saban and Samuels (2016) and Hessel and Hinton (2021) (forthcoming).

9 Stiegler is my silent interlocuter throughout this book as it was through his reworking of Heidegger's analytic of care in relation to the urgency of the Anthropocene that I awakened to it (Stiegler, 1998, 2013, 2016, 2019). I attempt throughout this essay to veer away from the many neologisms Stiegler creates to deepen his arguments for the sake of a beginning reader that may sadly dilute the richness of his text. See Daniel Ross's article "Care and Carelessness in the Anthropocene Introduction to "Reading of Stiegler and Heidegger" from a talk he gave at the University of Canterbury, Christchurch, May 11, 2018. Ross is a not only a translator (from the French) of Stiegler's works but also interprets/summarizes key aspects of Stiegler's thought.

10 Heidegger radically altered the direction of philosophical thought a century ago by introducing the centrality of *Sorge* in his existential analytic of *care* known through factical life experience. I discuss Heidegger's fundamental ontology at length in contrast to Jung's foundational ontology (such as Kant and Schopenhauer embraced) in Brooks, 2011. We might be tempted to note an echo of Heidegger's notion of care in the Jung's quotation I refer to above if Jung had not so ardently rejected Heidegger's thought. A big difference is that Jung is making an impassioned remark while Heidegger is building a philosophical edifice premised on factical life experience.

11 We can begin to see how Heidegger's fundamental ontology may be extended and particularized to include other alterities encountered in a differentiated humanity of beings within a widening swath of so called identities and isms to include race, gender (queer), age, status, and so on, a theme I weave throughout this book.

12 I particularize Ross's summary of Stiegler's definition of politicality (Ross, 2018, p. 7; Stiegler, 2019, p. 26) based on a reading of Heidegger's notion of care that corresponds to my use of the Lacanian subject's psychical structural movements toward trans-subjectivity developed further in Chapters Two, Three, and Four.

13 Traditional psychoanalysis is future oriented (teleological) and blind to the effects of catastrophic trauma that demand historical context beyond Oedipal and infant configurations. What was central for Jung was the teleological trajectory of the self's individuation while for Freud's aim was the teleological transformation of the pleasure principal by the ego (Brooks, 2016; Wallwork, 1991, p. 122).

14 The archetypes while self-constellating were not the same as the self but emanations *from the self whose center* Jung now implied was the "world soul," or the "empty center" *the archetypes pointed to* (Letters II, p. 259–260). In Chapter Three, I elaborate the crucial importance of the empty thing at the core of the split subject as the source or creative possibility in Lacan and Kristeva. Jung, however, associated the empty center to God or the God/self.

15 See *Gilbert Simondon Being and Technology* (2016) for a variety of essays that contextualize the intellectual influences found in Simondon's work as well as how contemporary thinkers are carrying his thought forward.

16 Simondon was embedded in the contemporary discourses on phenomenology, general systems theory, Marxism and Lacan's linguistic interpretations of Freud's opus and the birth of deconstruction. It is interesting to note that Simondon is reported to have been an assistant to Lacan but to what degree they influenced each other is left to our imagination (Scott, 2014, p. 8). He also referenced physics, biochemistry, physiology, embryology, sociology, cybernetics, and psychology in the development of his concepts.

17 Many of Simondon's texts remain untranslated from the French to this day. David Scott has translated and critiqued the latter third of Simondon's thesis titled *L'individuation psyche et collective* (1989) (Psychic and Collective Individuation, hereafter IPC). Any of Scott's translations from IPC are cited through Scott's text titled *Gilbert Simondon's Psychic and Collective Individuation A Critical Introduction and Guide*, 2014.

18 *Culture et technique* was reprinted in *Simondon, Sur la technique*, PUF Paris (2014) translated in 2015 by Olivia Lucca Fraser and Giovanni Menegallenotes in *Radical Philosophy*.

19 *On the Mode of Existence of Technical Objects* (*Du mode d'existence des objects techniques*) was the first section of Simondon's thesis published in 1958 and translated from the French into English in 2012, translated by Cecil Malaspina and John Rogove. Through Lacan's notion of the real, and Žižek's materialist

reading of it that we find an intersection with Simondon's theorizing ontogenesis as a basis for psychic and collective individuation. Žižek's rejects the dichotomy between the subject and its reality as Adrian Johnston succinctly summarizes his position thus: "The subject is "emergent in relation to the body" that is to say, such "immaterial" (or more accurately, more-than-material) subjectivity immanently arises out of a material grounds. Cogito-like subjectivity ontogenetically emerges out of an originally corporeal condition as its anterior ground" (Johnston, 2004, p. 231).

20 Stiegler leans heavily on Simondon's philosophical accounting of individuation after he read his works in 1986 (Stiegler, 2019, p. 74). Ross has argued that in Stiegler we find three reworkings of Heidegger critically engaged in the three volumes beginning with *Technics and Time I* (1998). The third reading of Heidegger engages the question and character of being through care centralized in the fate of the Anthropocene a concern continued through his remaining works.

21 According to Stiegler, we are in the gap between the Hyperindustrial Epoch that gave birth to the real of the Anthropocene whose impossible solution may be found through this new epoch he refers to as Neganthropocene. These ideas are fully elaborated in his latest text 2019. Stiegler died at age 68 in August of 2019.

References

Acka, U. (2017). Identity as the difference of power and the differing from being. *Research in Hermeneutics, Phenomenology and Practical Philosophy.* IX, 1, 300–320.

Badiou, A. (2003). *Saint Paul and the Foundation of Universalism* (R. Brassier, Trans.). Stanford, CA: Stanford University Press.

Bair, D. (2003). *Jung: A Biography.* New York: Little, Brown.

Brooks, R. M. (2011). Un-thought out metaphysics in analytical psychology: A critique of Jung's epistemological basis for psychic reality. *Journal of Analytical Psychology.* 56, 492–513.

Brooks, R. M. (2013). The ethical dimensions of life and analytic work through a levinasian lens. *International Journal of Jungian Studies.* 5, 188–199.

Brooks, R. M. (2016). The intergenerational transmission of the catastrophic effects of real-world history expressed through the analytic subject. In *Ethics of Evil Psychoanalytic Investigations,* 137–176, Eds. R. Naso & J. Mills. London: Karnac.

Butler, J. (2006). *Gender Trouble: Feminism and the Subversion of Identity.* New York: Routledge.

Chabot, P. (2003). *The Philosophy of Simondon Between Technology and Individuation.* New York: Bloomsbury Academic.

Christakis, N. A. (2019). *Blueprint the Evolutionary Origins of a Good Society*. New York and Boston: Little, Brown Spark.

Crapanzano, V. (1952). *Waiting the Whites of South Africa*. Toronto, London, Sydney, New York: Granada.

Frosh, S. (2015). *Psychosocial Imaginaries Perspectives on Temporality, Subjectivities and Activism* (S. Frosh, Ed.). New York: Palgrave Macmillan.

George, S. (2016). *Trauma and Race. A Lacanian Study of African American Racial Identity*. Waco, TX: Baylor University Press.

Giegerich, W. (2004). The end of meaning and the birth of man. *Journal of Jungian Theory and Practice*. 6, 1, 1–66.

Goodwyn, E. (2012). *The Neurobiology of the Gods*. New York: Routledge.

Gullatz, S. (2010). Constructing the collective unconscious. *The Journal of Analytical Psychology*. 55, 691–714.

Heidegger, M. (1999). *Contributions to Philosophy*. Bloomington, IL: Indiana Press.

Heidegger, M. (2001/1927). *Being and Time*. New York: Harper One.

Heidegger, M. (2010). *The Phenomenology of Religious Life* (M. Fritch and J. A. Gosetti Ferencei, Trans.). Bloomington, IL: Indiana University Press.

Hessel, W., & Hinton, L. (2021). *Shame, Temporality and Social Change*. London and New York: Routledge. Forthcoming.

Hinton, L. (2011). Unus Mundus – Transcendent truth or comforting fiction – Overwhelm and the search for meaning in a fragmented world. *Journal of Analytical Psychology*. 56, 3, 375–380.

Hook, D. (2008). Fantasmatic transactions: On the persistence of apartheid ideology. *Subjectivity*. 24, 275–297.

Hook, D. (2018). *Six Moments in Lacan*. London and New York: Routledge.

Johnston, A. (2004). Against embodiment: The material ground of the immaterial subject. *International Journal of Lacanian Studies*. 2, 230–254.

Jung, C. G. (1927/1970). Women in Europe. *CW*. 10.

Jung, C. G. (1947/1954). On the nature of the psyche. *CW*. 7.

Jung, C. G. (1936). Individual dream symbolism in relation to alchemy. *CW*. 12.

Jung, C. G. (1935). The Tavistock lectures on the theory and practice of analytical psychology. *CW*. 18.

Jung, C. G. (1973). *Letters of C.G. Jung*. II, 1951–1961.

Kiehl, E., Saban, M., & Samuels, A. (2016). *Analysis and Activism Social and Political Contributions of Jungian Psychology*. London and New York: Routledge.

Kristeva, J. (1987). *Black Sun Depression and Melancholia* (Leon S. Roudiez, Trans.). New York: Columbia University Press.

Kristeva, J. (1991). *Stranger to Ourselves* (Leon S. Roudiez, Trans.). New York: Columbia University Press.

Kristeva, J. (1995). *New Maladies of the Soul* (Ross Mitchell Guberman, Trans.). New York: Columbia University Press.

Kristeva, J. (2000). *The Sense and Non-Sense of Revolt: The Powers and Limits of Psychoanalysis, Volume 1* (Janine Herman, Trans.). New York: Columbia University Press.

Lacan, J. (1988). *Freud's Papers on Technique 1953–1954, The Seminar of Jacques Lacan. Bk.* Cambridge: Cambridge University Press.

Lacan, J. (2006). *Écrits: The First Completed Edition in English.* Translated with notes by Bruce Fink, in collaboration with H. Fink and R. Grigg. New York and London: W. W. Norton.

Lu, K. (2013). Can individual psychology explain social phenomena? An appraisal of the theory of cultural complexes. *Psychoanalysis, Culture & Society.* 18, 4, 386–404.

Lu, K. (2020). Racial hybridity Jungian and post Jungian perspectives. *International Journal of Jungian Studies.* 12, 11–40.

McGowan. (2016). *Capitalism and Desire.* New York: Columbia University Press.

McGrath, S. J. (2012). *The Dark Ground of Spirit Shelling and the Unconscious.* New York: Routledge.

Mills, J. (2018). The essence of archetypes. *International Journal of Jungian Studies.* 10, 3, 199–220.

Mills, S. (2016). *Gilbert Simondon Information, Technology and Media.* London and New York: Rowman & Littlefield International.

Mouffe, C. (1993). *The Return of the Political.* London: Verso.

Plomin, R. (2018). *Blueprint: DNA Makes Us Who We Are.* UK: Penguin Random House.

Ross, D. (2018). *Care and Carelessness in the Anthropocene Introduction to a Reading of Stiegler and Heidegger.* Christchurch: University of Canterbury.

Saban, M. (2020). Simondon and Jung: Re-thinking individuation. In *Holism Possibilities and Problems*, 91–97, Eds. C. McMillian, R. Main & D. Henderson. London and New York: Routledge Taylor & Francis Group.

Samuels, A. (1993). *The Political Psyche.* London and New York: Routledge.

Samuels, A. (2001). *Politics on the Couch.* London: Routledge.

Scott, D. (2014). *Gilbert Simondon's Psychic and Collective Individuation A Critical Introduction and Guide*. Edinburgh: Edinburgh University Press.

Simondon, G. (1989). *L'individuation psychique et collective*. Paris: Aubier.

Simondon, G (1992). *The Genesis of the Individual, Incorporations* (Jonathan Crary & Sanford Kwinter, Eds.). New York: Zone.

Simondon, G. (2012/1958). *On the Mode of Existence of Technical Objects* (Cecile Malaspina and John Rogove, Trans.). Minnesota and London: University Minnesota Press.

Simondon, G. (2014). *Sur la technique*. Paris: Presses Universitaires de France.

Simondon, G. (January/February 2015/1965). Culture and technics. *Radical Philosophy* retrieved from: http://www.radicalphilosophy.com/article/culture-and-technics-1965. Accessed 10/19/19.

Stavrakakis, Y. (1999). *Lacan & the Political*. London: Routledge.

Stiegler, B. (1998). *Technics and Time, I: The Fault of Epimetheus*. Stanford, CA: Stanford University Press.

Stiegler, B. (2013). *What Makes Life Worth Living: On Pharmacology*. Cambridge: Polity.

Stiegler, B. (2016). *Automatic Society, Volume 1: The Future of Work*. Cambridge: Polity.

Stiegler, B. (2017). What is called caring? Beyond the anthropocene. *Techné: Research in Philosophy and Technology*. 21, 2–3, 386–404.

Stiegler, B. (2018). *The Neganthropocene* (Daniel Ross, Trans.). London: Open Humanities Press.

Stiegler, B.(2019). *The Age of Disruption Technology and Madness in Computational Capitalism* (Daniel Ross, Trans.). Medford, MA: Polity Press.

Unless otherwise stated, the following are from the *Collected Works of C.G. Jung* (*CW*) London: Routledge & Kegan Paul/Princeton, NJ: Princeton University Press.

Wallwork, E. (1991). *Psychoanalysis and Ethics*. New Haven, CT: Yale University Press.

Webster, J. (2018). *Conversion Disorder: Listening to the Body in Psychoanalysis*. New York: Columbia University Press.

Žižek, S. (2008). *The Sublime Object of Ideology*. London and New York: Verso.

Chapter 1

Self as political possibility: subversive neighbor love and transcendental agency amidst collective blindness

> It is the last vestige of a dead world or the cradle of a shiny new one.
>
> Beryl Markham in *West with the Night*

Introduction

Carl Jung made a prophetic observation that spoke not only of the catastrophic effects of World War I but also foreshadowed a future whose terrifying remainders linger tragically today. From the ruins of a shattered Europe, he instructs us with the urgency of originary knowledge. "To really break with [a soul deadening] tradition," Jung said, one has to be "willing to risk everything for it, to carry the experiment with [one's] own life through to the bitter end, and to declare that [one's life] is not a continuation of the past, but a new beginning" (Jung, 1927/1970, para. 268). Even though peace and economic recovery appeared to be re-establishing itself in 1927 when Jung wrote this essay, the coming Great Depression of 1929 would soon unravel any sense of regained civility or stability in and beyond Western civilization. New and appalling levels of disregard for human life, including ethnic diversity would soon advance as economic instability would further give way to already rising extremist movements that would enable decades of uncritically held violence. It was from this moment in history that Jung was urgently speaking. The traditional ways of understanding and attending to the prevailing crisis of spirit were failing.[1] Indeed, the crises at hand arose from a carelessness of thought in the first place and the withdrawal of thought from the body. Collective blindness to a ruin that none of us

DOI: 10.4324/9781003136873-1

can escape, then and now contributed to the spread of what Bernard Stiegler refers to the "ordinary, everyday apocalyptic feeling—the feeling and the knowledge that something has come to an end" (Stiegler, 2013, p. 10).[2]

Jung described the inauguration of the subject (self) and redemption of a savaged Europe as being dependent upon one's capacity to surrender to the neighbor's plight, or as he put it—to take the step that Nietzsche's *Zarathustra* could *not* take, the step *toward* the "ugliest man, who is the *real* man" (1927/1970, paras. 268–271, my emphasis). The "real" as I am using it here is a term created by Jacques Lacan that is correlated with the effects of contingent traumatic events that shape human beings. That is, the self is contingent[3] upon its encounters with the real whose very definition lies in its utter *resistance to* symbolization and is therefore incomprehensible, unintelligible, and inarticulatable. While experienced as an alien force that suddenly penetrates us from outside of ourselves, the real touches us from within (one's psychology). The sensorial effects of the present trauma, therefore, aggravates my psychical scar tissue that has accumulated over time and resonates with all of the other times I have constituently failed to understand (what Heidegger refers to as existential guilt) what was happening to me—or my world. Encounters with the real will radically disrupt our coherent sense of reality. Put another way, the real as a transcendental dimension of unintelligibility is experienced through unbearable bodily intensities such as shock, horror, dread, anxiety, and the violent whoosh of emptying out (one's bowels, mind, stomach, vitality, or life force) while violently breaking through banal existence. For Lacan, *the neighbor is the real* (Žižek & Daly, 2009). What breaks through banality holds the potential for a different kind of knowledge that Heidegger referred to (following Kant) as authentic or originary knowledge from which we may begin view ourselves, our neighbor and world from a more vivifying perspective.

Jung contended that the self's telos was furthered through the principle of enantiodromia when encountering the real of the neighbor. Enantiodromia is a psychological process that occurs when the emergence of an unconscious opposing quality is integrated into the personality. Zarathustra, as the Nietzschian "Superman/Dionysian" figure was analogous with the Jungian self and the ugliest man represented his shadow opposite. Elaborating on this idea further, Jung stated: "The man that makes for growth is the ugliest man, the inferior man, the instinctive collective being, and that is exactly what he loathes the most" (Jung, 1998, p. 164). This step toward the real of the neighbor, Jung continued was generated within the individual from a "higher plane of love" and compelled one to break out of heretofore unconscious deadening social and psychological ideological restraints, as St. Paul had done (1927/1970, para. 265).

Let's take a deeper look into Jung's engagement with Nietzsche's text. Jung identified Zarathustra's moment of truth as culminating through his violent sensorial repulsion upon taking in the real of his neighbor. Leading up to this moment, Zarathustra finds himself on a path in a barren wasteland depicted as a valley of death that is devoid of all animal life (Nietzsche, 2012, pp. 310–311). Nietzsche describes the impending *face-off* as one that slowly registers through the protagonist's encroaching anxiety and darkening mood while pulling his awareness inward. "Then, however," Nietzsche narrates, "when he [Zarathustra] opened his eyes, he saw something sitting by the wayside shaped like a man, and hardly like a man, something nondescript. And all at once there came over Zarathustra a great shame, because he had gazed on such a thing" (p. 311). Zarathustra encounters the real of the ugliest man, his neighbor.

If only Zarathustra could have tolerated the unbearable intensity of his own terrible shame when faced with the horror of the ugliest man's *ex-sistence*[4]…a shame that momentarily evoked a deeply personal and ethical response to the impossibility of his neighbor's demand that is also, and this is a central point of this essay…crucially linked to the fate of his own dawning humanity. However, this is not the step that Zarathustra could take because the shame in witnessing the rawness of being human overwhelmed him. Let's follow the text with a sample of the ugliest man's retort to Zarathustra upon his failure to bear the shame that is evoked under the neighbor's disemboweling gaze:

> Thou thinkest thyself wise, thou proud Zarathustra! Read the riddle, thou hard nut-cracker,--the riddle that I am! Say then: who am_I_! –When however Zarathustra had heard these words, __ what think ye then took place in his soul? PITY OVERCAME

HIM; and he sank down all at once, like an oak that hath long withstood many tree-fellers....heavily, suddenly, to the terror even of those who meant to fell it. But immediately he got up again from the ground, and his countenance became stern. (Nietzsche, 2012, pp. 311–312).

In a single moment, we can see how Zarathustra's shame was rapidly converted to sternly masked pity, thus demoting my neighbor as fellow creature into *less than*.

This unconscious dynamic is played out ubiquitously in daily life such as when I mindlessly give my spare change to a nameless homeless creature in my neighborhood or other countless impersonal so called charitable gestures that momentarily absolve me from a more intimate or *dangerous* libidinal connection with the empty thing (*das Ding* or the enigmatic core of being/self). Our embeddedness within collectives is *both* a source of social belonging and deadening hegemonic control. We are (all of us) helplessly lulled in our human animal status that is lodged in a primal level of uncritically held immersion in our every day practices with others, what Jung referred to as "the herd," Heidegger described as *"das Man"* or Stiegler the "inhuman-being that we are" (Heidegger, 1927, p. 164; Jung, 1998; Stiegler, 2013, p. 132).[5] The collective hypnotic experience of *das Man,* however, *is* susceptible to sudden and meaningless eschatological disruptions that *may* compel us to decide a new way of being—where what once had seemed impossible becomes possible. Contemporary French philosopher Alain Badiou elaborates on this idea thus:

> There is only a particular kind of animal, evoked by certain circumstances to *become* a subject – or rather, to enter into the composing of a subject. This is to say that at a given moment, everything he is – his body, his abilities – is called upon to enable the passing of a truth along its path. This is when the human animal is convoked to be the immortal that he was not yet. (2001, p. 40)

In other words, something actually happens to us, a kind of radical contingency that violently pulls us down to our knees by revealing an inescapable and singular poignancy. If we can contain our unbearable libidinal intensities without going up in flames, possibilities that were here-to-fore unthinkable can reveal the obvious...that it is time *be* serious.

What then are the conditions within my intersecting worlds of experience and my own psychology that allow me to respond meaningfully to my own singular moment of truth? How do I come to acknowledge the enigma of my neighbor as an obligation to make myself accountable to myself and to others for what I say and do (Butler, 2005)? In this essay, I argue for a *notion of political action* that can emerge when the realities of what concerns us in our everyday lives becomes radically penetrated by a destabilizing threat to what we deeply care about. Such a destabilizing threat has the potential to completely alter how we care, think, practice, and creates a possibility for starting over again in the face of powerlessness from conditions where there is no hope.

In the process of writing this paper, I realized that I needed to expand my research approach into an interdisciplinary design in order to respond to the questions I pose in the introduction and throughout. As such, I focus on the themes that the questions evoke and engage in a sustained dialogue with those themes from different ways of knowing within academia (theory) and outside of it (the applied action that can occurs through collective inquiry). The disciplines I thematically engage are philosophy, psychoanalysis, and anthropology. My aim is not to bridge theoretical divides into a unified whole but to critically hold what is thematically relevant. While this research framework includes aspects of a traditional compare and contrast approach in addition to a critique of different thinking systems, it predominantly attempts to reach outside of those systems by looking creatively into new ways of investigating questions that are beyond traditional frames of understanding with the aim of attempting to rethink what it means to be a human subject amidst collective blindness in our moment of history.[6]

The narrative journey that follows does not provide the reader with closure to the questions posed but will, I hope, provide an impetus for further discourse. To this end, I engage with Slavoj Žižek's political theory as it relates to political subjectivity along-side of Badiou's characterization of the subject indelibly marked by an event of truth. I attempt to balance the theoretical and methodological rigor behind this notion of political action as it intersects the emotional, relational, and creative experiences of actual people engaging the real of the neighbor amidst a plague. Illustratively, I use a concrete example that arose *from* and in response *to* the catastrophic effects of the real of the AIDS pandemic in Portland, Oregon in the 1980s and 1990s from an autoethnographic perspective.[7] Autoethnography is a contemporary form of social research that attempts to understand the complexities of individuals among others and their unique struggles within the process of figuring out what to do, how to live, and essentially how to make meaning of an existence that has suddenly lost its foundation in the midst of a crises (Adams, Jones & Ellis, 2015). As an analyst/psychotherapist member of this forming community, I use my own experiences in conjunction with the oral and written histories of my immediate colleagues and long-term survivors in the study of the conditions under which the emergence of a community-based clinic run for and by the people living and dying of AIDS occurred. I portray a revolution of egalitarian-based care that emerged from a social void that cracked open and illuminated the real of AIDS.

Lastly, I wrestle with early Heidegger's secular reading of the Apostle Paul and the Christian revolution as means of engaging his formulations of authentic knowledge and its co-affectivity within group contexts. I incorporate distinct aspects of Badiou and Jung's use of Pauline doctrine to augment the discussion. Heidegger was interested in understanding what he referred to as the "factical life experience" or the here-and-now existence of Paul and the early Christian community he founded as it was shaped by their co-engagement with the event of conversion and eschatological rupture. I attempt to unthread certain intricacies of facticity to the extent that we might better understand how the Pauline subject of the Christian revolution might be relevant to contemporary emancipatory enterprises whose ontological ground (and transcendental agency) is rooted in authentic rupture.

Theoretical considerations of political subjectivity and action

Žižek offers a political theory that does not separate the subject from the social/political/historical forces from which it is embedded except through its particular encounters with the *real*. He views the symbolic structures the subject is always already inserted in *throughout life as the very conditions of possibility* for identity. This includes a polity that has failed to adequately recognize and/or come to terms with the crisis it is undergoing as was the case with the AIDS crisis. Indeed, the subject in Žižek's mind *is* a political possibility to be realized through the political act that can only occur when the subject encounters the real of a particular societal absence via the *lived* experience of disavowed others or those who live outside of society's material, emotional and/or social scope of recognition. *These are society's refugees who already live beyond the margins of public discourse, and while actively co-existing amongst us remain psychically invisible to the modes of influence that identify what a society values or not.*

For Žižek (following Lacan), such a traumatic encounter in turn reverberates with the subject's own internal core of emptiness that is reminiscent of the original birth trauma universal to us all. For the Lacanian subject, this original rupture occurs because of the intrusion of the big "Other" into the infant subject's seamless reality.[8] The initial encounter with the Lacanian real affords the subject with its first experience of the irreducible separateness from something "other" than itself and hence reverberates in the core of the subject throughout life in subsequent eschatological encounters. We can see this dynamic in play with Zarathustra's encounter with the residual "empty thing"—his neighbor the ugliest man. This foundational experience of lack activates the death drive that in turn stimulates fantasies of reunion with the lost object and/or generates symbolic investments (ideals etc.) in the world repeatedly throughout life (Brooks, 2016). Think of the death drive as a psychical "first responder" to trauma whose reflexive and deeply unconscious mandate is to turn inward and seek an originary oneness with my memorial "Other" to avoid annihilation at any cost.[9] Its mandate is not extinction but the prevention of death, what Žižek refers to as "that which persists beyond death"—that undead insistence to live on no matter what (2004, p. 33). From this understanding of the drives, we can see how the subject's capacity to intervene in the dialectical tensions born by the drives (activated by trauma) becomes the mechanism by which the human animal enters into the possibility of rising to a human subject status or alternatively remains compulsively linked to a terrifying undead object or both throughout life.

When the emerging subject encounters the real of death in the other who is reflecting back its own finitude—it is simultaneously exposed to the nothingness at the core of all beings and our vulnerability to subsequent encounters with it- *becomes* the "groundless ground" that connects us all and emerges in the face of the being's finitude (Nancy, 2012, pp. 26–28). It is on this basis of a "groundless ground" that Jean-Luc Nancy argues for a community (post Enlightenment) that is made up only of the network and interweaving of "shared singularities." On this, he states:

> Sharing comes down to this: what community reveals to me, in presenting to me my birth and my death, is my existence outside myself. Which does not mean my existence reinvested in or by community, as if community were another subject that would sublate me, in a dialectical or communal mode. Community does not sublate the finitude it exposes. Community itself, in sum, is nothing but this exposition. It is the community of finite beings, and as such it is itself a finite community. In other words, not a limited community as opposed to an infinite or absolute community, but a community of finitude. (pp. 26–28)

Nancy *is not disregarding* the historical shift *away from* communal ways of knowing that in the Western tradition through the Enlightenment had been dictated through the auspices of transcendental agents such as the church or other knowledge bearers who were cast in the role of one who is supposed to know (Giegerich, 2004).[10] Nancy is attempting to articulate a communal possibility that instead is informed through the *singular* experience of the *real* of death as it is held within a community of individual mortals (Nancy, 2012, p. 27).

This communal possibility occurs through the *individual's failure* to internally comprehend its own impending bodily disintegration. The real of death destroys the delusion of cohesive ontological ground. Science, the government, the love of God etc. will not save me from the inevitability of my death or restore a coherent reality in its stead. Instead, the rupture *becomes* the condition for the possibility for authentic self-relating in the world *with* others. Later, I will turn to Heidegger's secular reading of Paul and his followers as an example of such a counter-cultural possibility for our times, as I argue the emergence of Project Quest was during the onset of AIDS pandemic. The Pauline subject, according to Heidegger, shared a fidelity to the authentic retrieval of "facticity" amidst everyday living. Facticity in this sense was made possible through acknowledging the radical otherness (via the singular experience of the living Christ, in this case) that in turn committed the early Christian follower of Paul to be responsible to oneself and others while confronting the absolute enigma of being within a meaning giving process (what Heidegger would later refer to as *Ereignis*). It is crucial to underscore that a shared reality in this sense does not close-off death's unintelligibility (or excess) via communal fusion (perpetrated by unifying myths designed to restore delusional consistency) but is instead a space where a plurality of singular experiences *can* occur among the many within a shared ethos that does not distort the traumatizing effects of the real.

From this background, we can perhaps better grasp the singular manner in which the subject is *thrown* (in the Heideggarian sense) when encountering the real of a societal void or what Badiou has referred to as an "event of truth" (2001).[11] The event, for Badiou occurs when the subject experiences a break from established knowledge...a break that violently (following Lacan) "punches a hole" in what-ever the subject thought it knew about anything (Badiou, 2001, p. 43). Such a break exposes the subject to the experience of profound disempowerment (and/or dread, shame) promulgated by an encounter with the real at a societal scale. What defines the Badiouian subject is his/her fidelity to the truth-event over time, especially through the inevitable and tortuous trials of uncertainty, ambiguity, and ambivalence regarding what the "truth" is in the first place *and* the doubt if one is actually serving it.[12]

While Badiou and Žižek have their theoretical differences, they are unified in their use of the Lacanian real as their source of eschatological rupture. The real of Žižek's *act* or Badiou's *event* is irreducible to the situation induced by the rupture. Both embrace its violent nature (physical and/or psychical) and agree that through it life becomes worth living. While both root their political theory on rupture's possibility they differ greatly in their views regarding its relation to history and conception. For Badiou an event of truth can occur through exposure to the radical contingency of love (as in the case of St. Paul), the arts and science (including technology) in addition to politics. The situation of the AIDS plague, for example, may serves as an event of truth from which, I argue the work of love's possibility can occur through a community of care amidst unrelenting hopelessness. If the subject can retain a fidelity (in the Badiouian sense) to its truth (via working with the tensions of the drives without going up in smoke (imploding, splitting, etc.) in the face of profound uncertainty then the possibility for political action (the emergence of a community-based mind–body clinic), through love's fidelity...can occur.

The political act, returning to Žižek requires the subject to redefine himself at the very core of his identity (Žižek & Daly, 2009). In the language of Jungian Psychoanalyst Wolfgang Giegerich, in order to enter the land of the self, one has to go through a psychological (logical) death, the criterion being whether one has radically broken with his old identity or not—that is itself the goal (Giegerich, 1999, p. 17). Such a redefinition requires nothing less than a violent wrenching out of the indifference of everyday being that eventuates a decisive break from the symbolic order from which it occurs. It is this violent breaking away from tradition that makes the act political but the reason for the act is not.[13]

What drives the subject in a political act is personal (psychical)—to *hopelessly* resolve ones inner antagonism promulgated by reverberations of the empty thing—a kind of "death-driven singularity" throughout life (Santner, 2005, pp. 121–122). What makes the act political however is the subject's sweeping and decisive break with the hegemonic social link whose deadening authority has utterly failed. Social change of this order requires a willingness of the subject to fully recognize that *we are also the targets of its totalizing violence.* The subject's inner struggle that is reactivated by its identification with the neighbor's lack via the death drive *does not reinvest in a hope for a better world beyond loss and trauma.* Authentic rupture *instead,* and this is crucial for Žižek requires that the subject turn *toward* the real of the wound of its own trauma while retaining a fidelity to the hopelessness of the real of the neighbor's wound.[14] Eric Santner has defined love for the neighbor as the "singular force that first allows us to uncouple the [death] drive from its destiny" (2005, p. 124). The subject's pull to the real of the wound not only ignites the subject's responsibility to the other (echoing Emanuel Levinas) but radically distances the subject from the symbolic forces that have here-to-fore controlled it. With this act, the subject enters the void that functions as the epi-center of the social structure's unconscious and *joins the neighbor who is already there* (Žižek, 2011). The action of joining the neighbor is the actual expression of the subject's complete surrender to new iterative realization of our joined precarity (in the Butlerian sense) or what it means to be fundamentally human. Badiou views this revolutionary ontological ground as contingent upon the demolition of social distinctions that reinstall society on a more universal basis. This universal basis grounds the subject in a truth event that is linked to the real of multiplicity and universal equality (to which I will return below).[15]

Every political act disrupts the subject's investment with a social order that had once sustained it thus obliterating that which is most precious—our symbolic identity (McGowan, 2010, p. 26). One must be willing to not only define for oneself what is good but take full responsibility for one's belief, thus breaking away from the blind or resisting order (Žižek, 2013, pp. 1–8). Symbolic identity may be dependent upon my job, my financial security, my zip code, the good opinion of my family, friends or colleagues, and so on. Thus, and this is a key point in Žižek's politics, the relationship between the symbolic order and the real are reversed in priority depending on the subject's capacity to bear the fierce antagonisms of the death drive and by *denouncing a social order that condoned exclusivity*.

The revolutionary emergence of Project Quest: an illustration of neighbor love.

Over 25 years ago, I was co-leading a psychodrama residential retreat with medical psychologist Lusijah Marx and psychotherapist Graham Harriman and 28 participants living with AIDS at Doe Bay resort on Orcas Island. During the first night, one of our members (whom I will call Constance) began to menstruate in her sleep. The blood quietly hemorrhaged out of her body onto the mattress and floor throughout the night. We found her in a coma in the morning as we were gathering for the first session of the day.

Our entire community moved into action. Within moments, Constance was being carried on a mattress to one of our vans. Greg Carrigan describes the moment this way: 'We could all see our own death then and it was at the same time so healing because we were all [literally] lifting her [on the mattress] over us…she floated over the top of us.' We headed towards a colorful van decorated with a rough sketched hand-painted rainbow motif. One of the retreat participants, spontaneously started to play his flute and long soulful notes accompanied the somber procession to the van. We were quite suddenly thrown (in the Heideggarian sense) from the order of the everyday into a reality that we were already immersed but had somehow eluded us. That is, the ordinariness of our lives had quite violently been punctuated by the reality of Constance's blood, what that foretold, our powerlessness and responsibility to her impossible demand. Lusijah and Deb Borgelt (friend and volunteer) drove towards the ferry that would take them to a hospital off island. Next, I remember that Graham and I, half mad with fatigue were sitting on a sofa preparing to gather the group and instinctively holding each other's hands like a lifeline. Such a tender moment. We were all engulfed in a fierce eddy of unintelligible forces that were swirling around and through us. 'Are you ready? I said, looking into his eyes…"Yes,"' he said, and we stood up and moved into the gathering storm.[16]

In the brief vignette above, I attempt to describe the inexplicable horror of Connie's predicament that within an evanescent moment ignited a spontaneous collective expression of care.[17] What were the conditions that contributed to the collective and novel response to Connie's overwhelming need, and to the emergence of Project Quest itself? Whilst Žižek, Badiou and others have elaborated on the theoretical conditions under which human-being (subject, self) can be constituted by engaging the real of my neighbor, how does an *individual*'s response to a moment of truth (the real of AIDS) transition into a radical *collective* response to the neighbor who as it turns out is not only like me but now stands beside me? By standing beside my neighbor, I enter into a kind of strange kinship that irrevocably alters the course of my existence. In what follows, I attempt to answer the questions posed with both a linear and diachronic depiction of the evolutionary process of the Quest community. The Quest community sheltered a kind of intensified experience of life that allowed for radically individualized self-expressions to reorient not only the everyday existence of the individual but that of a forming community.

Project Quest was as co-founder Lusijah Marx stated it, *"the manifestation of the dreams of many people-and of the intense needs that were present in a dark and terrifying time."* The Quest community did not just suddenly appear. Quest's seed thought began in the early 1980s when Lusijah was focusing on formulating a dissertation topic concerning the hypnotic treatment of disease amidst the exploding AIDS crises. She was drawn to the idea formulating a treatment approach that incorporated the patient's mind/body response to the HIV virus about which little was known. She then designed an impressive Psychoneuroimmunological protocol in her study that incorporated key aspects of Eriksonian hypnotic guided imagery around the idea that the patient could improve their immune system's response against the encroaching HIV virus.

With her first "subject," Lusijah quite suddenly made a radical break from her own carefully designed protocol, a move that in my mind was a foundational step in what would lead to many more cascading and ever increasing novel departures from traditional models of care in response to the AIDS crises. Instead of following *her own idea* (endorsed by her dissertation committee) of what would be the best process of improving the patient's immune system, she (in hypnotic induction) asked the patient: *"What do you need at this time to help you heal?"* She did not define healing, nor did she describe a methodology from which healing (whatever that is) would occur. She left that up to the patient and she *followed* him or her. Immediately (and she was astonished by this), the patient dropped into the memory of one event after another about the terrible traumas that had occurred in their lifetime prior to infection. A similar response to the same question continued to occur with subsequent patients in the study. She began to realize that working with the protocol alone was insufficient. Each patient was so traumatized by their various psychological deprivations prior to a HIV diagnosis that their capacity to imagine or connect with an inner sense of resource was greatly impaired. In other words, each patient had turned toward their own real that the real of AIDS had opened (a primal wound) when asked what they needed for healing.

Given the immediacy of the crises, Lusijah suddenly knew that she needed to expand the therapeutic frame to include working within regular groups in addition to individual work so that *"deep healing work could occur."* Deep healing work became attending to both the everyday antagonisms of staying alive and hermeneutically engaging with one's psychology among others. Lusijah knew that she needed to secure a regular gathering place where meaningful connections with other affected people could be made because so many individuals were isolated, sick and/or dying alone. She recruited others within her immediate professional world one at a time. The lack of infrastructure in the city to care for the epidemic became clear. It is almost impossible to describe the feeling of the times. As Lusijah stated it:

> Those years were inspired-yet incredibly painful and sad. You never knew who would be the next to really get sick...or die. There were so many killer infections that could attack a weakened immune system like Kaposi's sarcoma-with its dark blotches, the telltale spots, or pneumocystis pneumonia where breathing became a total struggle, or CMV that would take your eye sight-leaving you blind, or MAC with a deep fatigue that made movement of any sort very difficult.[18]

Individuals who were infected with HIV disease were given not only a certain death sentence, but became societal pariahs fueled by terrifying fantasies and realities about the disease. Tabor Porter recalls the remarks made by his physician upon being diagnosed with HIV disease in the early days. *"He told me point blank that people like me would ruin the medical industry and that he couldn't help me or prolong my life but would try to make me comfortable."*

The death rate was astonishing and surreal. Porter describes the "general malaise" as ubiquitous. *"Everybody was dying"* and he knew he would be next. He continues: *"I never thought of myself as brave or even desperate at the time. It felt more like a dream when I look back. It did truly feel primordial."* Greg Carrigan describes his feelings in those days as vacillating between the daily unbearable intensity of not knowing if he would survive to see another day to the unexpected ecstasy of seeing a beautiful sky and pulling over in his car because he was uncontrollably weeping, so happy to be alive. *"Remembering those times now are like a burning scar."* Friends who had been healthy would suddenly hauntingly appear wasted and walking with canes in public spaces and/or suddenly disappear from everyday life. Porter describes how many men he knew either delayed being tested (and the tests were primitive and somewhat unreliable in the early days) or did not talk about their status at all. He describes the omnipresent sense of dread, fear, grief, and of feeling guilty for still being alive. Treatments (such as AZT) were either nonexistent or life threateningly toxic until 1996 when antiretroviral therapies (ART) first became available. HIV-positive individuals were afraid to tell anyone including family members they were infected creating an environment of intense isolation, despair, debilitating anxiety and terror. Others held onto their jobs with seriously declining health because there were no support systems yet in place. Porter describes how his boss fired him because *"he said he did not want to watch me slowly die."* These descriptions relay a feeling for the conditions amidst the social void created by the plague that Lusijah and others would enter and from which collaborations of care were continually generated.

Lusijah soon realized that in addition to the regular on-going group and individual therapy experiences already established, she also wanted to provide regular psychodrama retreat experiences as a way of enhancing communal cohesion. She asked me to help her as we had earlier trained together and were already co-leading non-HIV focused psychodrama retreats. The work shifted as a community of men and women living with HIV disease and AIDS continued to rapidly form through an ongoing venue of group-centered retreats and other forms of mind-body medicine that became available largely through volunteer efforts. Carrigan describes the comfort of being in those early groups with Lusijah this way. *"Sitting with other men who were also in survival mode waiting to die…Being in these early groups gave [me] something else to put [my] mind and energy into. As more people heard about Quest, the mind-blowing psychodrama retreats began."* The group venues had, in other words the effect of deepening and expanding community life, a momentum that was already in motion. Carrigan states it this way: *"Something about those retreats... making powerful in-roads...a powerful movement of doing our work productively...giving us something else to live for...a double edge where we all could see our own death and healing...it was important and real."*

Political subjectivity as I am outlining it here falls to me if I can recognize myself in the struggle of and with other(s) and freely assume responsibility for it by no longer relying on a useless transcendental agency (once believed to be outside myself) to save me or my neighbor in *my* stead. As Lusijah noted: *"For all who came together there was intensity-and a decision to be made...Is this [commitment to personal work] for me? Many were drawn together...some stayed, others left, and many died."*[19]

About this time, Lusijah and Lucas Harris, one of the study's original participants dreamed a shared dream on the same night. They each dreamt that they would start a healing center-together.[20] Lusijah was initially appalled. How could she trust this man who was a hairdresser with a 10th-grade education and 25 years her junior in such a major enterprise? She also knew that to enter into a collaborative enterprise with Lucas would deepen her commitment to a hopeless cause (in that there was no cure for AIDS) and it would also require that she open her heart so deeply to him and to so many others already living with and dying of AIDS that she would be violently uprooted even further from the comfort of her everyday world in all of its securities. There would be no turning back. Lucas would dedicate his remaining short life in support of the emergence of this center with a sense of purpose he had not yet experienced in his short life. Lusijah would leave behind a reliable income, her marriage, and the status of more traditionally minded clinicians and physicians in her professional world. In other words, Lusijah and Lucas completely walked away from a former frame of life that had protected them from regular exposure to the dangerous libidinal connections with their own deep selves.[21] Project Quest was founded in 1989 having established its 501c3 non-profit status.

Simultaneously, Graham Harriman, a young gay man with a new master's degree in psychology asked to be a part of what Lusijah and Lucas were forming. There was no money in it, Lusijah warned him but together they *"found a way"* for their work to be sustainable. Graham gave Quest a kind of needed accountability not only because he had natural administrative abilities (finding money) but also because as a gay therapist living with HIV disease he was more authentically rooted in the domain of what in Greek is called "*Ate,*" In his reading of *Antigone,* Lacan described *Ate* as the unspeakable domain of horror…that of being "in-between-two-deaths"…still alive but excluded from the broader communal world (Lacan, 1992, pp. 270–287; Žižek, 1999). On one side of the space in-between the two deaths is the subjective death experienced through the violent shock of becoming a stranger to myself. This could occur, for example, when I see an AIDS-related lesion forming on my face activating the fierce antagonisms of the death drive…to stay alive no matter what. On the other side is my impending actual bodily death against which I am now utterly and irrefutably powerless. The gay man infected with HIV or the Native American woman, as was Connie in the opening vignette, is already alienated from society because of their sexual or ethnic identity.

In this sense, the person diagnosed with HIV in the 1980s and 1990s was living a kind of collective double alienation ("double death") akin the "inner emigration" phenomenon described by Hannah Arendt in Germany leading up to Hitler's final solution. The emigrants in this case were not really emigrants but persecuted German Jewish citizens who behaved (congruently) as if they no longer belonged to the country they dwelt in and withdrew into a form of exile… "*a shift from the world and its public space*" (Arendt, 1968, p. 19). Privo Levi's evocation of the *Muselmann*—a "living dead" figure among the many in *Auschwitz* (Levi, 2015, pp. 83–85), Walter Benjamin's depiction of the *Odradek* figure in his reading of Kafka's protagonists (Benjamin, 2001, pp. 807–811), and Giorgio Agamben's figure of the *homo sacer* (Agamben, 1998) all contain a dimension of humanity that remains suspended in a kind of societal void amidst the ontic current of the everyday world. It is from such a background that Žižek (leaning on Lacan) and others have powerfully attempted to reformulate Freud's original figure of the *Nebenmensch* into a contemporary version of *the neighbor* who occupies the personal gap of *Ate* within the social gap described above.[22]

Graham fiercely wanted to be a part of building what was newly emerging as an *off the grid* community-based response to the needs of the people it was serving—an option that was not available elsewhere at the time. As he so poignantly states it today: *"We followed the needs of individual community members as they emerged by becoming intimately involved in each other's lives as the times called for that,"* This included expanding traditional clinical boundaries into more porous ones such as: being with individuals in the hospital and at home during illness, death, and dying times; taking phone calls at all times of the day and night; finding expensive hard to get medications through underground pipelines; cleaning up vomit and other bodily modes of care; participating in commitment ceremonies and/or other celebrations of all kinds sometimes including our own family members and so on.

Lusijah, Graham, and I co-led multiple residential and non-retreats in those early years of the pandemic. There were many times when we co-created new clinical responses to the unpredictable and unprecedented demands of retreat participants. The reformulation or creation of our methods was often in response to demands revealed in the raw dying of others alongside of a fierce and poignant desire to live fully. We laughed and cried hard and deep. The urgent need of participants to openly discuss their sexuality, desires, physical and psychological pain, personal life failures and fears of impending death within the retreat work exposed me to the narrowness of my own personal experience and professional training and often brought me to my knees in humility and shame.

I made some of my most egregious clinical errors in those days. How I practice today has been indelibly shaped by these foundational experiences where I was yanked away from an illusory grounding of (theoretical) certainty into a kind of human to human relating from which therapist(s) and patient(s) struggled together with the unbearable intensities beyond the safety of illusion. Furthermore, I was a white, privileged "breeder" woman (a hetero who had a child) in the middle of a predominantly gay plague oblivious to cultural nuances or to my own uncritically held biases and privilege. A now, close friend challenged me at one of the early retreats this way. He said: "What *do you know about AIDS, or about me and my sort of life at all? You live in your big house on the hill with your beautiful family and your four wheel drive mini-van and think* you *can help me?"* Lusijah and I were often the projective targets of individual projection as white women and so called breeder authority figures who were not

HIV positive, along with various transferences that were heightened by the palpability of death. We struggled with this material in the group while supporting each other. I was in psychoanalysis the entire time, a privilege that I now see was crucial for my own resilience and in analytic training.

Lusijah, Graham, and I continue to reflect today about what it was about the group work that contributed to the emergence of what became a kind of egalitarian community of healing, especially as it might be useful in our present turbulent global unrest. One crucial element we identified was a shared ethos that was greatly influenced by our shared psychodrama training an amalgam of the founder's foundational ideas about human rights. Briefly stated here, Jacob Levy Moreno (1889–1974) argued throughout his life that the individual's access to spontaneity and creativity was a key component to the possibility of living fully in a diverse world. In his inaugural text, *Who Shall Survive,* Moreno famously claimed that a real therapeutic process should have nothing less for its object "than all of humanity" (1953/1977). The singularity of the individual, therefore, could be translated into some kind of universality that was founded in one's innate access to creativity. Access to one's creativity levels distinctions between others by recognizing what is common among ourselves as peoples and at the same time does not disallow what remains irreparably separate. Moreno believed in the healing potential of groups and that group members therefore could be healing agents to each other if their barriers to their own creativity could be worked through. Furthermore, his methodologies in therapeutic group process included sociometric explorations that could enhance group cohesion by examining shadow dynamics. Cohesion is another illusory fantasy of ground but the process of working together with our projective fantasies as they arose in group process amidst the strangeness of the times was an intimate form of holding.

I will summarize the thread of ideas thus far elaborated that are salient to the notion of subject as political possibility (grass roots revolutionary) in response to the neighbor's plight. The political subject is one who has encountered the real of a particular societal void through the neighbor's unbidden appeal and thus is violently wrenched out of the indifference of banal existence. Such a vicious exposure to one's own ignorance and primal lack (via the empty thing, my own resonating deprivation) may also reveal a momentary glimpse into another dimension (the transcendental or what Heidegger refers to as authentic or primordial time) of what it means to be fundamentally human if one can bear the shame and humility. Only from such an engaged position can a singular moment of truth (novelty) be revealed in a penetrating flash of pure possibility and beginning. The subject's ability to respond to the neighbor's impossible demand is dependent upon a capacity to bear the fierce and terrifying libidinal tensions born by the drives when activated by a destabilizing reality. When the subject makes the fundamental choice to act, a new and terrifying space opens to everything (possibilities) through a heightened awareness of lived time. The cost is perpetual struggle, uncertainty, the radical loss of identity, and a decisive break with the empty abstractions (laws, traditions, ideological affiliations) contained within a social order that condones exclusivity.

In the following section, I engage selected readings of Pauline doctrine that illuminate how we may think about revolutionary response to the neighbor from our moment in history. I particularly focus on Heidegger's secular examination of the transcendental dimension of thought and the conditions for its collective or co-experienced possibility via factical life experience in the early Christian community.

Paul's subversive retroactive address

Paul the Apostle has been a figure of intellectual curiosity for some time and can be found in the historic works of Hegel, Comte, Nietzsche, Freud, Jung, and Heidegger, to name a few. The return to Paul in our present (post) modern epoch of heightened global uncertainty is not lost on a number of contemporary philosophical thinkers to include Critchley, Santner, Agamben, Badiou and Žižek. Critchley considers the secular return to Paul's address as a demand for a "new figure of activism" motivated by political despair in an age of moral relativism and uncritically held consumptive global capitalism (Critchley, 2012, pp. 156–157). Badiou's secular reading of Paul also searches for a "new militant figure" that can deploy a contemporary critique of global Capitalism run amuck. The Pauline subject for Badiou radically breaks from the external authorities (*Weltanschauung* and other political abstractions) of his time by turning instead toward "the Voice" that personally summoned him to his "becoming-subject" in order to follow a new order of truth (2003, p. 18). The Badiouian event of truth is potentially available to all (not just religious leaders) and as such becomes a renewed foundation of universalism through which Paul can offer us revolutionary strategies founded in an egalitarian ethos to radically confront our present contexts. In other words, each of us has the potential to authentically engage each other in novel and life giving ways that reach beyond the nullifying norms in which we are all embedded.

Unlike Heidegger or Badiou, Jung did not conduct a formal critique of Paul's works. In 1957, following the second world war, Jung claimed that both Jesus and Paul were prototypes of those who by "trusting their inner experience, [have therefore] gone their individual ways in defiance of the world" (1964/1957, para. 536). Jung was concerned about how easily an individual's own ego-consciousness could be dominated by his "purely animal *participation mystique* with the herd" (1928/1931 para. 150), or the "mob" psychology that he discusses at some length in the Zarathustra seminars (1998, pp. 247–253). Loving or caring for one's neighbor, in contrast to "the soulless herd animal," relied on the capacity for self-love and that depended upon the ability to differentiate oneself (ego) from that autonomous realm within (1998, p. 248, 1946, para. 444). Individuation from this perspective also engendered a kind of "kinship libido," an instinct in ordinary people that sought human connection and a sense of belonging together (para. 445).[23] Jung appears to be elaborating on a form of kinship libido he thought was missing amidst the devastation, unmitigated violence and spiritual crises that followed the Great War. He writes:

> In this reality we are no longer differentiated persons but are conscious of our common human bonds. Here I strip off the distinctiveness of my own personality, social or otherwise, and reach down to the problems of the present day, problems which do not arise out of myself-or so at least I like to imagine. Here I can no longer deny them; I feel and know myself to be one of the many, and what moves the many moves me...for here it is not the individual will that counts but the will of the species. (Jung, 1927/ 1970, para. 261)

What was at stake for Jung was a component of being human that held a species together through a capacity to care about and take responsibility for the fate of humanity in contrast to the collective blindness of the herd. Badiou and Jung converge briefly here on the point of emphasis of deploying self-love toward others, in direct opposition to other (non-secular) interpretations guiding the individual to empty oneself out (a form of "narcissistic pretension") in devotion to the other (Badiou, 2003, pp. 88–92).

Badiou views "the law of love" as the universal (available to all) and a vehicle of faith working through love tirelessly.[24] While Heidegger did not extensively elaborate on love's message in his reading of Paul, he did emphasize the centrality of "self-knowledge" as the means of interpreting how one might comport oneself within the early Christian community and in wider worldly contexts. The conditioning ground for such self-knowledge or what Heidegger referred to as facticity, required the individual to confront the radical enigma of being human while being accountable to oneself and others in everyday living. In other words, conversion experiences are possible for all (not only potential apostles) within the context of everyday life (on the road to Damascus) and lodged within ruptures of all intensities if only we have the sensibility to notice, engage, and heed.

Jung correlated the experience of the religious transformation of *Saul's conversion to Paul* as a psychological process he called enantiodromia, you will recall from this essay's introduction, that was the basis for his principle of compensation. On enantiodromia, Jung stated: "This characteristic phenomenon practically dominates conscious life: in time an equally powerful counter-position is built up, which first inhibits the conscious performance and subsequently breaks through the conscious control" (Jung, 1964/1957, para. 709). He used Paul's vision of Christ and conversion experience as an example of psychic phenomena that he associated with his later reformulation of the psychoid archetype (1956/1957, para. 1586, 1587). While the conversion from Saul to Paul might have been experienced suddenly and seemingly out of the no-where, for Jung it was not an eschatological breakthrough as is theorized in Badiou, Žižek or Heidegger's ontology.[25] Jung's Saul was in the grip of a sudden conversion because of an enantiodromia process that had all along been controlled by the organizing and arranging activities of the psychoid archetype whose center was the world soul (1947/1954, para. 393; 1921/1971, paras. 709, 712). That is, Saul's conversion to Paul was an enantiodromia between an inferior man (or inferior function) and the Jungian self (echoing the ugliest man and the rope-walker in Zarathustra) (1998, vol. I, p. 1021). Thus, the step that Zarathustra could not take in Jung's view occurred because he was rejecting his own inferiority that was projected onto the neighbor and neighborhoods.

Heidegger, Badiou, and Jung found in the Pauline corpus a point of departure that deepens and extends their particular philosophical systems that can then be abstracted or generalized into a kind of universal reality. Heidegger's reading of the Pauline subject and the early church allowed him to work out his own conception of the phenomenological method in departure from his teacher Edmund Husserl who is generally considered to be the father of philosophical phenomenology. In what follows, I attempt to unthread salient aspects of these inextricably bound components of facticity to the extent that we might better understand how Heidegger's political subject of the "Christian revolution" is relevant to contemporary grass root sub-versive enterprises with a keen eye toward the phenomena of co-affected facticity in group contexts (Heidegger, 2010, p. 96).[26]

Heidegger's contemplation of Paul's address

The vehicle for Heidegger's extensive engagement with Paul's texts was a series of lectures entitled "Introduction to the Phenomenology of Religion" that he conducted in 1920–1921 in Freiburg (2010). Heidegger gave these lectures during the immediate aftermath of the First World War amidst the massive collapse of established forms of knowledge, morality, and of everyday life. Empires and monarchies were disintegrating and there was a scrambling for territorial control and movement toward nationalist tendencies that heightened already prevalent ethnic racisms. Societies were breaking down, inflation was on the rise, and there was a general sense of disillusionment, unrest, and uncertainty (Gerwarth, 2016). Not only was the extended European continent ensconced in crises, but philosophy itself was experiencing a serious identity crises since the collapse of Idealism (a turn away from the attempt to theoretically systematize all ways of looking at reality) from which metaphysics would emerge as an ontology. Prior to the death of Hegel, philosophy had been situated as the central point for an absolute unification of thought and as such encompassed everything, including various academic disciplines within itself as one system. It was from this backdrop of a shattered European continent and philosophical tradition that Heidegger would distinguish himself from the traditional ways of philosophizing with a method that radically shifted away from a reliance on the presuppositions of his tradition in general (specifically Husserl's phenomenology of consciousness). He would transform phenomenology into a hermeneutics that strove to understand human being in its enigmatic *original* ground as it was constituted through crises (2010, pp. 58–59, 1925/1992).[27] He sought to temporalize the transcendental and recover a pre-theoretical level of experience he claimed had been lost in the entire Western philosophical tradition but could be understood in "factical life experience." Thus, he focused on the every-day life and struggles within the Pauline community as it was shaped through their co-engagement with the "living experience of the resurrected Christ" in support of his analysis of the temporality underlying existential phenomenology (p. 84). Heidegger engaged Paul's letters (specifically the interpretation of the First and Second Epistles to the Thessalonians) from a sensual/poetic state of reflection demonstrating a method of factical philosophizing. What this means can be better understood if we break down a few of Heidegger's central components of facticity below; throwness of being (crises), sense meaning making possibility, transcendental structures of authentic knowledge and time/historicality.

Heidegger's early study of Paul focused on the means in which human being and meaning are thrown together and the incumbent need and ability to come to grips with world's turbulence. In *Being and Time* (1927/1962), Heidegger would replace the oblique phrase "factical life experience" with another term "*Dasein*" that signifies the throwness of human existence or Being.[28] Coming to grips with one's world through factical life experience has more to do with engaging the multiple dimensions of sense meaning-making possibilities (via ruptures) that enable one to be one's own self through participation and involvement in the world, what Heidegger would later refer to as care (*Sorge*) (Heidegger, 1927/1962). Care in this sense does not mean a solicitous (mindless) turning toward the crowd (*das Man*) out of an anxiety to belong but instead is an expression toward others that is generated from a central component of the self's authenticity. We never experience ourselves as separate from the many modes of relationality, yet it is to our self-world that we are radically thrown when encountering the real. These worlds or modes of experience in which the self is always imbedded include the actual concrete environment, the shared world with other beings within various social milieus and self-world (*Umwelt, Mitwelt, Selbstwelt,* respectively) (Sheehan, 1986, p. 316).[29]

Paul's conversion into a religious/political revolutionary occurred within a society that upheld social inequality, slavery, and imperialism amidst the reigning military despotism of the Roman Empire (Badiou, 2003). The Christianity that Paul founded, according to Heidegger was not the religion of a historical Jesus of "pre-given forms of religion" as was practiced by the Jewish Pharisees. Paul's religion instead came to him from the authentic knowledge of facticity that arose from his conversion [or "original enactment"] through which he experienced a moment of "living in spirit" [through his risen son in an evanescent moment] (Heidegger, 2010, pp. 53, 84–85). Authentic knowledge is not the same thing as "theoretical cognition" prescribed by authorities relying on historical religious dogma (exclusionary legal categories determining who can belong and how) and rites (circumcision, dietary laws) (Heidegger, 2010, pp. 53, 84–85, 88–89, 101). How can we understand the transcendental structures of conversion further? In *Being and Time*, Heidegger would refer to this call of conscious as *Dasein* calling to itself from where it is not, "from beyond me" (1927/1962, H 275). Being is both caller and called. He elaborated the call this way:

> In its "who", the caller is definable in a "worldly" way by *nothing* at all. The caller is Dasein in its uncanniness: primordial, thrown Being-in-the-world as "not-at-home" – the bare "that it is" in the nothing of the world....it is something like an alien voice. What could be more alien to the "they," lost in the manifold world of its concern than the Self which has been individualized down to itself in uncanniness and been thrown into the "nothing." (H 276)

To recap, an alien voice from and beyond myself calls me to myself potentially out of the deadening grips of *das Man* into experience of foundational lack. Simon Critchley economizes these passages into a self that is divided between two nothings "a nothing of the world [on one side] and, on the other [side], the nothingness of pure possibility revealed in the being-toward-death" (Critchley, 2015, p. 72). From this perspective, we may consider Paul's conversion experience as throwness through the real of his lack (or inauthenticity, nullity) into the gap between the two nothings. On one side was the illusory grounding (a vacancy) within his everyday (religious) practices (*das Man*) to an awareness of pure possibility through which there were no guarantees except death. Unlike the religious interpretation of conversion where Saul becomes Paul in relation to God, Heidegger's self (or Being) moves toward itself or converts, individuates, becomes itself in relation to the shocking awareness of the two nothings.

We can see the parallels of the Heideggarian self-divided between nullity and that of the self-divided between the two deaths in Lacan's depiction of *Ate* as applied to being encountering the real of AIDS. In either depiction, the self as throwness absorbs the violent shock of feeling alien to itself whose authentic home is revealed as primordial emptiness (core of enigma) against a horizon that holds both radical possibility *and* certain death. Being, then is potentially something (versus nothing) *against* its lack. Heidegger described the existential lack to which one is exposed in throwness as guilt, not in the sense of one's moral failures toward society etc. but more in the existential sense of emptiness or powerlessness at its core (Heidegger, 1927/1962, H 286). Only through this exposure to and potential appeal of conscience, taking in or receiving the call and finally understanding and retaining a fidelity to its rigorous hermeneutics may one have a glimpse of what it means to *be* human and a greater sense of its pure possibilities.[30]

Thus, conversion required that Paul make a decisive break from the ideologies (laws, traditions, symbolic order) that deadened him toward his own authentic knowledge (in his case, the risen Christ), a pre-condition of factical life experience "constitutive for Christian religiosity" (2010, p. 85). Paul's conversion necessitated a radical break *from* the traditional adherence to religious law *toward* an inclusive ethos founded on factical life (Paul's proclamation) through which categories of belonging (traditional rites and relying on outside authorities for knowledge of any sort) became obsolete. The factical life of the early Christian *began* with a declaration to living the object of this proclamation—living the "authentic *dynamic of sense*" through which the possibility for authentic knowledge may be known through imminent experience (2010, p. 91). On this Heidegger stated:

> Now it must be shown that Christian religiosity lives temporality. What meaning communal worldly and surrounding worldly relations have for the Christian must be understood and if they do, in what way? Christian factical life experience is historically determined by its emergence with the proclamation that hits the people in the moment, and then is unceasingly alive…Further this life experience determines, for its part, the relations which are found in it. (p. 83)

Early religious experience can be seen in this light as a continual process of "reinventing oneself" or taking over one's own *throwness* that allows for momentary glimpses into the basic underlying structure of one's life and in one's relations with others. These glimpses into what really matters can allow one to be curious in novel ways, extend one's critical thinking into creative territory and compel one to try things out that her-to-fore had not been in one's frame of reference.

The primary mode of expression through which factical knowledge (or meaning making possibility) was made known was through the senses, mood and the like. Factical knowledge was transcendental and therefore could not be comprehended through rational means. The prevailing mood of facticity described by Paul was of "entering oneself into the anguish of life" (p. 66). The Pauline subject did not reinvest in a hope for a better world devoid of loss and trauma but instead struggled to retain its own vulnerability and to that of its neighbor with a comportment of resilient and unrelenting struggle. Struggle was promulgated by the "urgency of time" and characterized by absolute distress, anguish, weakness, and suffering ("wavering in sadness") within an ongoing worldly surround of uncertainty and oppression (pp. 80, 79, 101, 90). Facticity and throwness were irreducible elements of the experience of Being and the question of its individuation. Individuation in this sense came at a cost, heightened anguish and

almost if not abject hopelessness.[31] The Pauline subject was not bound
in hope for a future outcome but instead was engaged in the everyday
work of living authentic thought with others, what Badiou refers to as
faith tirelessly working through love (Badiou, 2003, p. 92).

Heidegger recognized various modes of facticity within the early
Christian struggle that were indissociably linked to everyday temporality and original time. One of Heidegger's early philosophical
breakthroughs was a notion of being human that was constituted not
only in time but *was* time itself. For early Heidegger, temporality *was*
the expression becoming oneself through a meaning making process
(Heidegger, 2010, p. 72). Time in this dimension was not a linear
progressive telos in that it had nothing to do with a subjectivity that
was constituted through a past that continued to effect the present
and one's future horizon. We see such a notion of time in Freud's
conception of *Nachträglichkeit* a form of retroactive constructivism, a
term he first used in 1895 in the *Project for a Scientific Psychology*
(Freud, 2001). Jung, on the other hand favored a notion of imminent
critique that privileged interpreting emergent psychic phenomena as
relevant to the present neurotic attitude of the patient.

Both Heidegger and Jung regarded immanent experience as a
fundamental necessity for understanding although from very different problematic. For Heidegger, Being's possibility is always and
already there (although intrinsically hidden) or *what I already am*—a
necessary and universal (*a priori*) feature of facticity (1925/1992). In
these early musings, Heidegger was developing a theory of time that
was syncopated through being's experiential movements that pro-
vided a kind of *original* unity of the past, the present, and of the
unknowable future except through the certainty of one's death.[32]
Original experience in this sense could only be inaugurated through a
diachrony of ruptures within an evanescent moment (such as Paul's
conversion experience) from which one may more reflectively grasp a
deeper sense of what it means to *be* human, what Heidegger referred
to as, originary, primordial, or authentic temporality (Heidegger,
2010, p. 50, 73, 83; Hinton, 2015, p. 365).

From this theoretical backdrop, let us return to the shocking scene
in the vignette above where Connie began to bleed out on her mattress during the night in the Quest retreat. When Connie's unconscious and bloody body was discovered in her room the next

morning, she was met with an immediate and novel collective response that was undirected by any one person, something akin to
Jung's depiction of kinship libido. There were few words. She was
gathered up by a creative force greater than our own whose tender
and life-saving action sprang forth from the horror of her imminent
death. Half ruined on her mattress, she was suddenly and tenderly
lifted over our heads in a whoosh of movement that floated her toward the van, accompanied by a mournful flute rhapsody. We knew
what to do for her and how to be with each other in an unfolding
collective movement that was eerily dreamlike and timeless. This
experience resonates with Heidegger's phenomenological depiction of
the co-effective expression of Being he referred to as "having become"(2010, pp. 65–74). Heidegger was temporalizing Kant's transcendental structures of knowledge by extending authentic knowledge
of the individual *into the communal milieu* (pp. 70–73).

Having become did not arise from a "homogeneous field of relations" but rather flowed through the being of one among other
beings, what Heidegger referred to as a "unity of a diversity" (p. 64).
As he stated it: "[T]heir having become is their Being now" (p. 66).
Mind in this sense was *a prior* (universal) openness, meaning giving
and existence itself. This is not a cult mind. Authentic knowledge
"must be of one's own" from which a sense of having become among
and with others was possible (p. 72). Hence, the Pauline subject unites
living thought in this sense with action. Badiou refers to the labor of
living thought with action as love (Badiou, 2003, p. 92).

Heidegger's references to enigmatic or "authentic" knowledge that
arose out of the complexities of everyday life (vulgar temporality) in
the early Christian were co-mingled with the surrounding world in its
seemingly enmeshed yet distinct temporalities. He elaborated (2010):
"Christian life is not straightforward but rather broken up: all
surrounding-world relations must pass through the complex of enactment of having-become, so that this complex is the co-present, but
the relations themselves and that to which they refer, are in no way
touched. Who can grasp it, should grasp it" (p. 86).

And further:

That is, while still living amongst others in the surrounding world,
the early Christian gives up all worldly means and significances

and yet fights his way through. Through the renunciation of the worldly manner of defending oneself the anguish of his life is intensified...is almost hopeless. (p. 87)

The Pauline subject cannot live in a static bubble of illusory solidarity. What makes the early Christian *revolutionary* is a capacity to be an ordinary person in a diverse world among others while retaining a relationship with one's self. What divided the subject was an irreducible relatedness to its animal/being status that is dependent on metaphysical rupture (real) to awaken it to a fuller possibility. The divided Pauline subject, according to Heidegger surrendered to the living real of rupture by retaining a fidelity to its meaning giving process within the concrete reality of everyday life. In so doing, he/she straddled the ontic and ontological divide thus forgoing any illusion of certainty or stability by forgoing the seductive allure of symbolic investments (false Gods) that compromise a fidelity to authentic self-engagement.

We must remember that Paul's entire Christian movement was founded on the rupture versus continuity of Judaism. Paul's letters were militant doctrines sent to small communities that had converted. Anyone could convert whatever their background and were considered as fully practicing equals in contrast to the more hierarchical traditions and practices of other Judeo-Christian sects of the time where clear distinctions were made between the Jew and Greek, slave and freeperson, man and woman, authority and follower. What defined the Pauline subject was not the strict observance of religious law, but a fidelity to subjective truth among others who shared this ethos while living ordinary life. Critical to Heidegger's depiction of the Pauline revolutionary is the impossibility of coherence among a world whose frame of reference is other to authentic self-reflection.

Discussion: transcendental agency and emancipatory revolution

There are three basic structural elements contained in Heidegger's depiction of the early Christian emancipatory revolution that are relevant enhancements to my thesis of self as political possibility in today's world. They are:

1. Singular rupture;
2. The hermeneutic of authentic knowledge and its conceptual extension to my neighbor, neighborhood and world;
3. The on-going everyday work of taking concrete responsibility to the object of my calling with and among others from which a new egalitarian ethos may emerge.

The first element requires an encounter with the real of some sort whose effects obliterate the illusory markers of cohesion and coherence that I have heretofore narrated myself around. Jacques Derrida refers to this dimension of phenomenology as a "spectral" presence or haunting component of lived experience that is neither in the world nor in consciousness but becomes available to the subject through rupture (Derrida, 1994, p. 6–10). The bottom drops out. What haunts me now catches up with me and I am thrown into a free fall. Saul's rupture appeared to be psychical, an encounter with the real of Christ's resurrection that radically disrupted his identification as a conservative Jew. Lusijah encountered the real of the AIDS epidemic and the social void of care in her own neighborhood that resonated with her own psychical deprivations.

The political subject in the second structural element must remain actively engaged with the real of the trauma that becomes the condition for the possibility of authentic self-relating in the world with my neighbor. The hermeneutics of living thought (transcendental) exposes me first to my own enigma *and then* I may grasp its significance to my world with a renewed or novel sense of responsibility toward it. Hence, the basis for critique of any kind includes a spectrum of thought that is inaugurated through an encounter with the real (itself transcendental), through which the subject may in a hermeneutics of reflection aim or intentionalize the object of its trauma. Traditional psychoanalysis is usually concerned with the individuation of the individual. Self as political possibility instead incorporates the many dimensions of meaning-making possibility that arise from the various concrete and enigmatic traumatic encounters within the social and other environmental milieus one mindlessly engages every day. At this stage, what emerges is an idea, an imaginary picture of possibility or action that springs out of the individual's deficit or enigmatic core in reverberation to the empty thing that has been antagonized by the rupture exposing me to my neighbor's lack. In psychodramatic terms, the protagonist is warming up to its concrete purpose that has not yet been realized in the world.

The third element involves *the work of taking concrete responsibility* to what I am now awakened and manifesting it somehow with and among others. We can see the parallels to Heidegger's depiction of early Christian factical life experience and that of Project Quest's co-affected response to the AIDS plague. The work task of the Quest community was to provide and maintain a community of care for and by the people who were suffering from AIDS amidst a world health crises devoid of sufficient authority. Lusijah was the initial visionary for what would later emerge into a co-created community grounded in a common egalitarian ethos. Solidarity existed only in moments of transcendent experience that lifted and informed individuals or sometimes groups of individuals toward a kind of concrete action that often furthered its collective purpose. By way of closing, I need to underscore Heidegger's deep and abiding insight into the pre-vailing anguish experienced by the early church community as the pre-condition of facticity that could also heal it. Healing does not imply a separation from suffering's reality but the contingency (Kant's insight) through which we may momentarily "be" other, with another or many others through the ecstatic *traces* of transcendent knowledge in the shared labor of being human.

Après coup

We are witnessing the heightening collapse of global democracy (founded on hermeneutics for and by the people) into an emerging form of governance whose motivational apparatuses are devoid of humanist and/or planetary considerations, what Naomi Klein refers to as "disaster capitalism" (Klein, 2009). In such a surround, economic gain and uncritically held consumerism are the reigning discourses and *nothing* else is real or guided by any principles of reason or other means of knowledge. The "nothing," as philosopher Catherine Malabou states it is the "absolute undoing of being human, of the historical and of the principle of [pure] reason…because with no reason, there is no reason at all for one thing to happen rather than another" (Malabou, 2016, p. 145). Nothing remains, in other words when the significance of being human disappears and we are not even certain to what or whom we are at the mercy of much less how to think about it.

Das Man for Stiegler today *is* the media, and through it the social networking enterprises that perpetuate a feeling that we live in an ongoing "present" along with the loss of tradition or the historicality against which we may access what really matters to us. Such a loss at its extreme can manifest in a feeling of nonexistence without a self-reflective capacity from which one may engage another possibility (Stiegler, 2013). We can sense the mounting danger of the arrival of a wholly other kind of global catastrophe amidst the vacuum of global leadership whose aimlessness does not lead us toward the work of thinking a new order of care now or toward the future. These catastrophic threats to our world are generated from human enterprises that have become contemporary autonomous dispensations of being (such as the mindless stupidity of our world leaders, ruthless despotism, uncritically held scientific advances, economic greed, global capitalism, ecological crises, technological developments, abjection of social injustices, etc.) and are spinning out of our control. The real of the neighbor is an idiom of cultural distress—an outcome of what has become estranged from knowledge in these real world processes. Cultural distress can also be known through encounters with the neighbor who carries this excess as a result of cultural negation in the face of mass inequality and injustice perpetuated in its many subversive forms.

We cannot rely on an outside agency to come to our rescue. The mounting fatigue from bearing the sense of impending apocalypse and its unintelligibility can reduce any of us to the banality of the soulless herd and inflame our passion for ignorance. Or the felt sense of urgency can singularly awaken a political self to the transcendent features of human experience revealed through the assault to what one truly cares about. From our moment in history, we need a new hermeneutic and knowledge basis from which we can engage the enigma of being human with a strategic eye toward a sustainable future.

Notes

1 French philosopher of the time, Paul Valéry made a similar observation by stating, "everything essential in the world has been affected by the war [...]. The Mind itself has not been exempt from all this damage. The mind is in fact cruelly stricken; it grieves in men of intellect and looks sadly upon itself. It distrusts itself profoundly" (Valéry, 1962, pp. 307–308), first seen in Stiegler (2013, p. 135).

2 Stiegler's vast philosophical project attempts to illuminate the underlying symptoms of global consumer capitalism which nullifies, he argues those whom it advertises it liberates. In this text, *What Makes Life Worth Living on Pharmacology*, 2013, Stiegler offers a theoretical cure for what he refers to as crises of the mind and spirit in our moment of history through the *pharmakon* of technics. Technics (organized, inorganic matter, or originary tools now technology) is the cause through which humanity is sickened by itself yet offers us a cure to our suffering and novel possibilities. Technology, he asserts has been repressed in philosophical consideration and cannot be separated from what constitutes being human.

3 Contingency as I am using the term here is related to the Kantian notion of the power to *be* other (via being delivered over to ecstatic traces of transcendent knowledge), a topic I return to throughout this essay.

4 I am using the term "ex-sistence" in the vein of Lacan's usage via Heidegger. The Lacanian subject is engaged in a constant process of projecting itself out onto the world subject (and it's others) and into the future thereby seeking the "extra knowledge of being" that is constituted through such horrific encounters with the real of other's being and that is a desire to know nothing, or a "passion for ignorance" (Lacan, 1998, p. 121). We can see this struggle to *know* and *not know* myself being played out through the other's desire in Zarathustra's shame, a shame that is demoted into a pity that deadens the possibility for a shared humanity… "the axe that felleth slays thee" (Nietzsche, 2012, p. 314).

5 Heidegger (1927/1962, p. 164) interchanges the *Das Man* with the "They" and/or "Inauthentic man or "they" [Average Man]. For example, he stated: "The 'who' is not this one, not that one, not oneself [man], not some people, and not the sum of them all. The who [impersonal] is the neuter, the 'they' [*das Man*]."

6 I have elsewhere described various modes of interdisciplinarity with a particular bias toward what Talvatie and Ihanus refer to as an interfield approach to my own research (Brooks, 2014, pp. 619–622; Talvitie Ihanus, 2011). This article exceeds the scope of my earlier approach. There are many definitions of multi, inter, intra, and transdisciplinarity that abound in the literature review. See this article for a relevant example (Darbellay, 2015).

7 Autoethnography (AE) is an anthropological term used to describe a contemporary form of qualitative research involving self-observation within the context of ethnographic fieldwork. AE uses the researchers critically held personal experiences in relation to and with the experiences of others within a particular field of study. AE emerged as a social research method in opposition to traditional

theories and practices in the mid- to late twentieth century. These theories and practices tended to uphold totalizing ideals contained by universal truths (sweeping overarching dogmas) about peoples and cultures that we still see today in cultural critiques.

8   The big Other is a manifestation of the symbolic realm. The symbolic realm is the complex network of society's explicit and implicit messaging conveyed via media, language, etc., and is always in the background of things. The big Other is often personified by a single agent such as the initial caregiver, my government, the God who watches over me from "out there," my psychoanalytic orientation, my genetic heritage, and so on.

9   Elsewhere, (Brooks, 2016) I have elaborated on the theoretical import of the death drive and super-ego development in clinical work and am particularly influenced by post-Lacanian thinker Adrian Johnston who extends its efficacy most notably in *Time driven metapsychology and the splitting of the drive* (2005).

10 Jungian Analyst Wolfgang Giegerich has richly elaborated on the historical shift from public (communal) ways of knowing to the singularity of felt experience as a means of self-formation in our present age in "The End of Meaning and the Birth of Man: An Essay about the State Reached in the History of Consciousness and an Analysis of C. G. Jung's Psychology Project," *Journal of Jungian Theory and Practice*, 2004. That is, the burden of consciousness in our present epoch (depicted by the so-called death of an all knowing God or outside authority that is located out there) falls upon the individual who is not separated from the public sphere and its processes but embedded within it. Like Lacan, and Badiou, Giegerich considers the emergence of the self to be inexorably bound to the world in its utter realness to include history, culture, technology, politics, economics, climate, etc.

11 Heidegger's concept of *thrownness* or "being thrown" into the world bears further explication as it a crucial (and ubiquitously used) concept (linked to other) that has acquired specialized significance in twentieth-century continental philosophy and remains relevant as a point of departure for later thinking. *Dasein* (being there, or presence) for Heidegger is a thrown projection (in the present) in the world. Basically, being human is always already found or disclosed through the arbitrary experiences of existence. Being thrown is an opportunity for *Dasein* to confront its personhood that is accessible via ongoing concrete encounters with everyday experiences with others.

12 I am thankful to Ladson Hinton for nuancing this thought with me.

13 For Badiou and Žižek, it is the rupture that makes life worth living (McGowan, 2010). Walter Benjamin claimed, as he was fleeing Nazi persecution that it was only through the utter ruins of a once sustaining foundation that a dimension of possibility for social change could occur.

14 While both Badiou and Žižek consider the event and act (respectively) to be a potential site for subject formation, they have different ideas about how this happens. Badiou's event introduces novelty while Žižek's act is correlated to the death drive and its endless repetitive call to return to the experience of primal loss (rupture).

15 One of the primary differences between the contemporary continental philosophical thought and that of Jung's foundational ontology has to do with ground. For Jung, there was unitary reality that was the ground of all phenomena (collective unconscious) beneath the workings of the archetypes whose center, he implied was the world soul (1947/1954, paras. 388, 393). For Jung, there was an outside vantage point or objective perspective of reality or a transcendental ground through the world soul whose emissary to the self was the psychoid archetype. Heidegger held that *Dasein* (or human existence) did not have itself as its own basis and was therefore not objectified, what instead Heidegger referred to as ontological ground (Brooks, 2011). Existence was continually interpersonally and socially constituted through everyday engagements with phenomena amidst temporal reality via traumatic engagements in the world as could be understood in transcendental structures of experience. These engagements would *throw* the individual into what he referred to as the "clearing" where moments of truth could be disclosed amidst the banality of everyday life. The clearing as such had a transcendent quality (being brought from nothingness) but was not a foundational ground as there was nothing behind or underneath it like in Kant's noumenal realm, or that we find in Jung's epistemological basis for the psyche. Later Heidegger would retain his interest in the authentic nature of existence but more in being's relation to its ontological ground of meaning or thought.

16 All of the named persons in this essay have graciously given me their permission to share this story and use their names in this paper: Deb Borgelt, Lusijah Marx, Greg Carrigan, and Graham Harriman (retained 2015–2016). Deb Borgelt presently is the Recovery Support Services Manager for Native American Rehabilitation Association of the North West (NARA). Greg Carrigan is a successful fine artist in Portland Oregon. "Constance" is not the real name of the woman who eventually died in the AIDS epidemic. Tabor Porter is a successful jeweller and metal-smith in Portland, Oregon. Today, Project Quest is now known as the Quest Center for Integrative Health, having expanded in 2000 to include all people affected by illness and chronic pain. Lusijah a medical psychologist and clinical director of QCIH and remains a primal force there. Graham is the Director for the Treatment and Care Program for the Bureau of HIV at the NYC Department of Health and Mental Hygiene.

17 The task of accurately narrativizing the real of the epidemic is impossible. I acknowledge the limits of grasping the unintelligibility of trauma, or articulating experience based on the ethereal quality of individual or collective memory, and of my own personal limitations and biases as a reporter. Writing this section was an emotional process for me and for the participants of this study. Lusijah Marx, Graham Harriman, and I are in the process of writing a text whose audience will be less focused on psychoanalytic community but toward a mental health and social services community. This article arose as my first attempt to articulate experiences that are by definition inarticulatable thus drawing on a cross

interdisciplinary theories and practices in addition to Analytical Psychology with the psychoanalytic community in mind.

18 Lusijah Marx, personal conversation, January 9, 2017

19 Lusijah Marx, personal conversation, January 9, 2017.

20 Lucan Harris died when he was 30 years old in the spring of 1996, only months after the release of the anti-viral medications that might have saved his life. I was with him when he died. Prior to his death, Lusijah and I directed Lucas in a deeply moving psychodrama where he enacted his death scene. He influenced me, the life of my family and many other individuals unfathomably.

21 I am reminded of this advertising slogan written by Rob Siltanen, writer of Apple's 1997 "Think different" Campaign when I think of the ethical turn both Lusijah and Lucan took when founding Project Quest: "Here's to the crazy ones. The misfits. The rebels. The troublemakers. The round pegs in the square holes. The ones who see things differently. They're not fond of rules. And they have no respect for the status quo. You can quote them, disagree with them, glorify or vilify them. About the only thing you can't do is ignore them. Because they change things. They push the human race forward. And while some may see them as the crazy ones, we see genius. Because the people who are crazy enough to think they can change the world, are the ones who do." I am grateful to Ted Leonhardt for guiding me to it.

22 See Žižek, Santner and Reinhard (2005). This timely text directly focuses on the theme of the neighbor and its authors philosophically engage alterity in deeply complex and distinct essays suggesting a new theological configuration of political theory.

23 "Kinship libido" is a term that has acquired some traction in post Jungian parlance even though Jung did not develop the concept with much specificity including its political implications. From a savaged Europe (1946), Jung seemed to be mourning our capacity to rehabilitate the human "instinct" of neighbor care that he noted was present once among the early Christians and was now lost. As will be seen further in this essay, Heidegger developed the concept of "having become" among the Pauline Christians that is similar to the feeling of what Jung is conveying in kinship libido, but its source is not instinctual. Heidegger's source of having become is transcendental, i.e., unintelligible, *a priori* and available in moments of throwness.

24 Badiou richly translates Paul's definition of love to be "the living unity of thinking and doing," or "that working through love" and as such becomes a new law open to everyone who retains fidelity to the Christ-event (of truth) (Badiou, 2003, pp. 86–92).

25 I am relying on a philosophical perspective of eschatology versus eschatological beliefs held through much of Western theological thought more traditionally associated with a total "end" for humanity. Heidegger focused on the inner experience of eschatology as he applied it to the factical life experience from his own extensive engagement with Paul's texts. Thus, he transformed the idea of the Christian eschatological experience of a second coming of the Messiah through

Paul's texts and contemporary theological usages *into* a phenomenological use (Lup & John, 2013). Heidegger sought to find a more primordial bases of early Christian life than was expressed here-to fore in teleological conceptions of history as we can see in his attempts to temporalize the transcendental structures of knowledge (a post Kantian move). For Paul, and the early Christians, there was no gradual unfolding progress of universal history. Instead, we are held captive to the ever-present spectacle of the eschatological event, a phenomenon that replaces and exposes this lack of theoretical meta-ground (Brooks, 2016). Heidegger's eschatological perspective of the future can be contrasted to the teleological view through which Jung (individuation) and Freud (via ego-psychology) oriented their psychologies. Teleology within this perspective implies a developmental emergence of not only of psychological structures but also of sociopolitical events and whole nations (persons and peoples) that are also governed by an unfolding progressive and predictable telos.

26 There are many theoretical threads of interest in Heidegger's Pauline study that are well beyond the scope of this essay. I do not cite the biblical references that Heidegger actually translated himself from the original Greek. My central focus here is to explicate aspects of facticity that may illuminate our understanding of the metaphysical aspects involved in the formation of an egalitarian ethos from which emancipatory collectives can form and inform.

27 While Heidegger retained the Husserlian phenomenological reduction as part of his hermeneutics, he rejected the Husserlian transcendental ego (or his transcendental phenomenology of consciousness) in favor of focusing on the hermeneutical phenomenology of facticity that was not a locus of consciousness (Heidegger, 2010, pp. 3–21; Sheehan, 2015, p. 44).

28 I do not conflating the experience of a human being engaging in its everyday world of things and activities (what Heidegger referred to as ontic reality) with the *mode of Being* that Heidegger refers to as *Dasein* throughout his works. Being for Heidegger was an ontological characterization of throwness. See footnote 12. In this paper, I use the terms "being human," "self," or "subject" interchangeably with Heidegger's notion of *Dasein,* not in an attempt conflate whole intellectual frameworks in one blind sweeping movement but more to highlight very specific points of similarity beyond distinct disciplinary perspectives that may be useful in engaging the research questions imbedded in each section of this article.

29 Later Heidegger emphasized the reciprocal relation of *Dasein's* need for meaning and meaning giving's need for being and the tensions between passive submission versus active sustaining of that need (*Ereignis*) (Sheehan, 2015, p. 59). We can see in this description of *Ereignis* a kind of foreshadowing of the Lacanian drive tensions already discussed above, a topic for another essay.

30 Being, in other words always lags behind its possibilities and we are always in its debt (Heidegger, 1927/1962, H 284, 289). Or in the words of poet Keith Johnson, "Life begins like a tangled ball of wool, it begins with nothing and ends with nothing." See: https://www.poemhunter.com/poem/a-good-yarn/

31 Badiou describes Paul's view on hope to be an expression of tenacious and ob-
    stinate imperative in the pursuit of justice, an enduring fidelity through an ordeal
    for which there is no expected reward and no future goal but the work of love
    (Badiou, 2003, pp. 93–97).
32 While both Jung and Heidegger leaned on Kant in their distinct formulations of
    what accounts for transcendental knowledge, their outcomes are quite different.
    The referent and from which transcendent knowledge could be ascertained for
    Heidegger was through authentic rupture (random and meaningless events) that
    penetrated the individual amidst his/or her everyday existence among others
    (socially constructed within a temporal reality). For Jung, the dispensing source
    of meaning possibility for the self was primordially given from the objective
    unconscious (world soul) via the psychoid archetype dependent upon the in-
    dividual's capacity to derive meaning from their symbolic presences (individua-
    tion). While both theorized a kind of unifying transcendental ground it was from
    very different problematics. See footnote 15. I have elsewhere elaborated at
    length on the differences between these two problematics, see Brooks (2011).

References

Adams, T., Jones, S. H., & Ellis, C. (2015). *Autoethnography Understanding Qualitative Research*. New York: Oxford University Press.

Agamben, G. (1998). *Homo Sacer: Sovereign Power and Bare Life* (D. Heller-Roazen, Trans.). Stanford, CA: Stanford University Press.

Arendt. H. (1968). *Men in Dark Times*. New York: A Harvest/HBJ Book.

Badiou, A. (2001). *Ethics an Essay on the Understanding of Evil* (P. Hallward, Trans.). London and New York: Verso.

Badiou, A. (2003). *Saint Paul the Foundation of Universalism* (R. Brassier, Trans.). Stanford, CA: Stanford University Press.

Benjamin, W. (2001). *Selected Writings: Vol. 2* (H. Zohn, Trans.). Cambridge, MA: Harvard University Press.

Brooks, R. M. (2011). Un-thought out metaphysics in analytical psychology: A critique of Jung's epistemological basis for psychic reality. *Journal of Analytical Psychology*. 56, 492–513.

Brooks, R. M. (2014). Accounting for material reality in the analytic subject. In *Behavioral Sciences in Dialogue with the Theory and Practice of Analytical Psychology*, Ed. L. Huskinson. Basel and Beijing: MDPI.

Brooks, R. M. (2016). The intergenerational transmission of the catastrophic effects of Real world history expressed through the analytic subject. In *Ethics of Evil Psychoanalytic Investigations*, Eds. R. Naso & J. Mills. London, UK: Karnac.

Butler, J. (2005). *Giving an Account of Oneself*. New York: Fordham University Press.

Critchley, S. (2012). *The Faith of the Faithless Experiments in Political Theology.* London and New York: Verso.

Critchley, S. (2015). The null basis-being, or between two nothings: Heidegger's uncanniness. In *Interpreting Heidegger,* Ed. D. O. Dahlstrom. Cambridge: Cambridge University Press.

Darbellay, F. (2015). Rethinking inter and trans disciplinarity: Undisciplined knowledge and the emergence of a new thought style. *Futures.* 65, 163–174.

Derrida, J. (1994). *Specters of Marx.* New York and London: Routledge.

Freud, S. (2001). *The Complete Psychological Works of Sigmund Freud Vol. I.* London: Vintage Publishing.

Gerwarth, T. (2016). *The Vanquished Why the First World War Failed to End.* New York: Farrar, Straus and Giroux.

Giegerich, W. (1999). *The Souls' Logical Life.* Frankfurt am Main, Germany: Peter Lang.

Giegerich, W. (2004). The end of meaning and the birth of man: An essay about the state reached in the history of consciousness and an analysis of C. G. Jung's psychology project. *Journal of Jungian Theory and Practice.* 6, 1, 61–65.

Heidegger, M. (1925/1992). *History of the Concept of Time Prolegomena.* Bloomington and Indianapolis: Indiana University Press.

Heidegger, M. (1927/1962). *Being and Time* (J. Macquarrie and E. Robinson, Trans.). New York: HarperOne.

Heidegger, M. (1929/1997). *Kant and the Problem of Metaphysics* (R. Taft, Trans.). Bloomington and Indianapolis: Indiana University Press.

Heidegger, M. (2010). *The Phenomenology of Religious Life* (M. Fritsch and J. A. Gosetti Ferencei, Trans.). Bloomington and Indianapolis: Indiana University Press.

Hinton, L. (2015). Temporality and the torments of time. *Journal of Analytical Psychology.* 60, 3, 353–370.

Johnston, A. (2005). *Time Driven Metapsychology and the Splitting of the Drive.* Evanston: Northwestern University Press.

Jung, C. G. (1927/1970). *Women in Europe. CW.* 10.

Jung, C. G. (1928/1931). *The Spiritual Problem of Modern Man. CW.* 10.

Jung, C. G. (1946). *The Psychology of the Transference. CW.* 16.

Jung, C. G. (1947/1954). *On the Nature of the Psyche. CW.* 8.

Jung, C. G. (1956–57). *Jung and Religious Belief. CW.* 18.

Jung, C. G. (1964/1957). *The Undiscovered Self (Present and Future). CW.* 10.

Jung, C. G. (1998). *Nietzsche's Zarathustra: Notes of the Seminar Given in 1934–1937* (J. Jarrett, Ed.). London: Routledge.

Klein, N. (2007). *The Shock Doctrine: The Rise of Disaster Capitalism*. New York: Picador.

Lacan, J. (1992). *The Ethics of Psychoanalysis 1959–1960: The Seminar of Jacques Lacan Book VII* (D. Porter, Trans.). New York and London: W. W. Norton & Company.

Lacan, J. (1998). Encore the Seminar of Jacques Lacan Book on Feminine Sexuali*ty, The Limits of Love and Knowledge, 1972–1973* (B. Fink, Trans.). New York and London: W. W. Norton & Company.

Levi, P. (2015). *The Complete Works of Primo Levi: Volume I*. New York and London: W. W. Norton & Company Ltd.

Lup, Jr., & John R. (2013). 'Eschatology in a Secular Age: An Examination of the Philosophies of Eschatology of Heidegger, Berdyaer and Blumenberg' retrieved from: scholarcommons.usf.edu/edx/4532

Malabou, C. (2016). *Before Tomorrow Epigenesis and Rationality* (C. Shread, Trans.). Malden, MA: Polity Press.

Markham, B. (1942/1983). *West with the Night*. New York: North Point Press.

McGowan, T. (2010). Subject of the event, subject of the act: The difference between Badiou's and Žizěk's systems of philosophy. *Journal of Critical Psychology*. 3, 7–30.

Moreno, J. L. (1952/1977). *Who Shall Survive?: Foundations of Sociometry, Group Psychotherapy and Sociometry*. Beacon, NY: Beacon House INC.

Nancy, Jean-Luc. (2012). *The Inoperative Community [Community]* (P. Connor, L. Farbus, M. Holland, & S. Sawhney, Trans.). London and Minneapolis: University of Minnesota Press.

Nietzsche, R. (2012). *Thus Spoke Zarathustra*. San Bernardino, CA: Simon & Brown.

Santner, E. L. (2005). Miracles happen: Benjamin, Rosenzweig, Freud, and the matter of the neighbor. In *The Neighbor: Three Inquiries in Political Theology*. Chicago and London: The University of Chicago Press.

Sheehan, T. (1986). Heidegger's 'Introduction to the phenomenology of religion', 1920–21. In *A Companion to Martin Heidegger's 'Being and Time'*, Ed. J. J. Kockelman. Lanham, MD: Center for Advanced Research in Phenomenology and University Press of America.

Sheehan, T. (2015). Facticity and Ereignis. In *Interpreting Heidegger*, Ed. D. O. Dahlstrom. Cambridge, UK: Cambridge University Press.

Siltanen, R. (1997). 'Think Different' retrieved from: https://www.forbes.com/sites/onmarketing/2011/12/14/the-real-story-behind-apples-think-different-campaign/2/#5881d72f7e56

Stiegler, B. (2013). *What Makes Life Worth Living on Pharmacology*. Cambridge, UK: Polity.

Stiegler, B. (2014). *Symbolic Misery Volume 1: The Hyperindustrial Epoch*. Cambridge, UK: Polity.

Talvitie Ihanus, J. (2011) On neuropsychoanalytic metaphysics. *International Journal of Psychoanalysis*. 92, 1583–1601.

Unless otherwise stated, the following are from the *Collected Works of C. G. Jung (CW)* London: Routledge & Keagan Paul/Princeton, NJ: Princeton University Press.

Valéry, P. (1962). The European. In *History and Politics*. New York: Bollingen.

Žižek, S. (1999). *The Ticklish Subject: The Absent Centre of Political Ontology*. London and New York: Verso.

Žižek, S. (2011). *Living in the End of Times*. London and New York: Verso.

Žižek, S. (2013). *Demanding the Impossible*. Cambridge, MA: Polity Press.

Žižek, S., & Daly, G. (2009). *Conversations with Žižek*. Cambridge, UK: Polity Press.

Žižek, S., & Delpech-Ramey, J. (2004). An interview with Slavoj Žižek 'on divine self-limitation and revolutionary love'. *Journal of Philosophy & Scripture*. 1–2, 32–38.

Žižek, S., Santner, E., & Reinhard, K. (2005). *The Neighbor: Three Inquiries in Political Theology*. Chicago and London: The University of Chicago Press.

Chapter 2

From leper-thing to another side of care: a reading of Lacan's logical collectivity

Introduction

In the present essay, I conceptualize the psyche-social dynamic of *trans-subjectivity* that itself is a precursor to the possibility of a collective in-dividuation or what Jacques Lacan obliquely referred to as "collective logic." This concept is related to what Heidegger described as "having become" (or later *Augenblick*), Gilbert Simondon as "trans-individuation, " and Derek Hook as "trans-subjectivity" (Heidegger, 2010, pp. 65–74; Hook, 2018, pp. 86–114; Lacan, 1945/2006, pp. 197–175; Simondon, 1992, p. 248).[1]

I elaborate a notion of "trans-subjectivity" through a reading of Lacan's 1945 essay entitled "Logical time and the assertion of an-ticipated certainty" whereby he delineates three iterative moments of logical time toward a culminating expression of a collective truth, or "logical collectivity" (Lacan, 1945/2006, pp. 197–175). While Lacan utilized the allegory of the prisoner's dilemma to illustrate his thesis, I use a clinical vignette from a Project Quest therapy retreat to ela-borate the symbolic processes underlying the movement between *inter-* and *trans-*subjective logic and the expression of a shared so-lution to the dilemma posed. Rarely does Lacan use the term "trans-subjective" and he does not do so in his 1945 essay. I borrow Derek Hook's use of this term from his own substantial reading of Lacan and trans-subjectivity (Hook, 2013, 2018).[2]

DOI: 10.4324/9781003136873-2

Self as political possibility

This essay is the second of two, the first entitled "Self as possibility: subversive neighbor love and transcendental agency amidst collective blindness" (Brooks, 2018). Before fleshing out the present thesis, I must briefly summarize crucial aspects of the first on whose shoulders this paper stands. Self as political possibility, as I am viewing it here can be seen as the enunciation of the "struggle to articulate the *I* with the *we*" amidst "blind [collective] stupidity" and a relationship to an impossible future and a past that is not one's own (Ross, 2018, p. 7; Stiegler, 2019, p. 26).[3] That is, the political subject is inaugurated not only through its own becoming (psychical individuation) but also through the emergence of a novel collective individuation (Brooks, 2018).

"Self as political possibility" was in part an auto-ethnographic study of the psyche/social conditions that contributed to the birth of a non-profit clinic called Project Quest in 1989 during the height of the AIDS pandemic. I engaged the philosophical and psychoanalytic thought of Jung, Žižek, Badiou, and Heidegger in formulating my thesis for co-effective individual and collective individuations. Quest's emergence was not an anomaly but serves as an example of how encountering the singular real of the wound of contemporary existence amidst massive entropic collapse (or collective disindividuation) may awaken us to something we truly care about, thus activating subversive expressions (thinking, actions, artistic productions) of care that may culminate in collective individuations (Stiegler, 2019, pp. 29–30). There are *basic structural elements* that contribute to self-formation in relation to others that have the potential to mobilize a group toward collective action. These collective actions resist and invert abusive dominating norms toward new expressions of care. I did not use the term "trans-subjective" in the earlier paper nor did I conceptually develop its role toward collective individuation, which is the focus of the present essay.

I now summarize three of these elements that form the background of the present paper. First, the subject engages a singular rupture, in this case a vicious exposure to one's own situation by engaging with the reality of the AIDS pandemic. As such, the subject is affected by the collision between the contingency of their own temporality and the incontingency of existence. The subject is brought to his knees, and if he can bear the fierce libidinal tensions activated by this destabilizing reality, a new and terrifying space opens to a heightened awareness of lived time through which a singular moment of truth may be revealed in a penetrating flash. Second, if the subject remains actively engaged with the reality of his dilemma, he may grasp its significance allowing him to make a fundamental choice to act on behalf of himself *and* his world with a new sense of responsibility: "I am not alone." "There are others like and not like me who share this dilemma." Third, the subject commits to an ongoing everyday struggle of taking concrete responsibility to the object of their truth with and among others so that a new egalitarian ethos may emerge beyond its own future. "I am dying, but what I labour for now may contribute to a better life for those I leave behind." In other words, the coin of this realm is not directed to my personal retirement plan but toward a society of care for which I make my sacrifice.

The cost is perpetual struggle, uncertainty, the radical loss of identity and a decisive break with empty abstractions contained within a social order that condones exclusivity. The work task of the Quest community, for example, was to provide and maintain a community of care for and by the people who were socially isolated because they were afflicted with a deadly disease amidst a world health crisis devoid of sufficient authority/resources in a climate of terror and violent discrimination. The times were dark as well as illuminating. Solidarity existed only in those trans-subjective moments that lifted and informed individuals and sometimes groups of individuals toward a kind of concrete action that often enough furthered its collective purpose (Brooks, 2018, p. 68).

Connie's blood and Lacan's notion of logical collectivity

Prefatory note: Half of the individuals attending the particular retreat in the following vignette are dead and all were HIV positive and/or living with an AIDS diagnosis. Highly Active Antiretroviral Therapy (HAART) would not become widely available in the US until the mid- to late-1990s. The so called "working through" the repercussions of the following incident of Connie's bleeding out occurred in sessions after she was taken off the island and became a focus of therapy in a variety of striking ways after the retreat. There were, of course, many trans-subjective moments that evolved in the multiple group processes of all kinds that led to the actual founding of Project Quest. What informs my clinical interpretative assumptions throughout this essay, now almost 30 years later, are culled from recollections, process notes, artefacts, and other materials collected from auto-ethnographic research I conducted with my colleagues and others who attended this retreat in the early years of the plague.

Lastly, the protagonist of this essay is the *subject*. The Lacanian subject is the *unconscious discourse of and with the Other*, as we will see.[4] I use various gender fluid pronouns for the sake of narrative clarity. The composite narrative I generate about this incident is delivered in a chaotic flux congruous with the discourse of self-formation and informed by the work we did together over years.

Clinical vignette

Almost 30 years ago, I was co-leading a psychodrama residential retreat with medical psychologist Lusijah Marx, newly graduated psychotherapist Graham Harriman and 28 participants living with AIDS at Doe Bay resort on Orcas Island. During the first night, one of our members (whom I will call Constance) began to menstruate in her sleep. The blood quietly hemorraging out of her body on to the mattress and floor throughout the night. We found her in a coma in the morning as we were gathering for the first session of the day. Our entire community moved into action. Within moments, Constance was being carried on a mattress to one of our vans. Greg Carrigan describes the moment this way: "We could all see our own death then, and it was at the same time so healing because we were all [literally] lifting her on her mattress, over us…she floated over the top of us." We headed towards a colourful van decorated with a hand-painted rainbow motif. One of the retreat participants, spontaneously started to play his flute, and long soulful notes accompanied the sombre procession to the van. We were quite suddenly thrown (in the Heideggarian sense) from the order of the everyday into a reality that we were already immersed but that had somehow eluded us. That is, the ordinariness of our lives had quite violently been punctuated by the reality of Constance's blood, what that foretold, our powerlessness and responsibility to her impossible demand. Lusijah and Deb Borgelt (friend and volunteer) drove

*towards the ferry that would take them to a hospital off the island.
Next, I remember that Graham and I, half mad with fatigue, were
sitting on a sofa preparing to gather the group, instinctively holding
each other's hands like a lifeline. Such a tender moment. We were all
engulfed in a fierce eddy of unintelligible forces that were swirling
around and through us. "Are you ready?" I asked, looking into his eyes.
"Yes," he replied. We stood up and moved into the gathering storm*
(Brooks, 2018, 55).

The first structural moment of time, that of the subject

Nobody alive today remembers who found Connie's unconscious
body in her bed. Dark red menstrual blood continued to drip out
from under the covers, still coagulating on to little pools on the floor.
At first sight, it looked like a crime scene. The smell of her blood filled
the room. The sight of her bleeding out presented *each of us* with our
own dilemma. Lacan's first logical gesture begins the moment the
singular subject engages the evidence of an existing dilemma, what he
refers to as "*the instance of a glance*" (Lacan, 2006, p. 204). The kind
of subjectivity that develops in the first logical moment Lacan refers
to as "noetic," "impersonal," and "independent" from others (ibid,
pp. 204–205). Instantaneously, the sight of *Connie's blood* evokes a
singular wrenching away from the banality of the everyday into
"fulgurating" time (ibid, p. 167). A memory from a forgotten history
may "flash up" in the Benjaminian sense in moments of danger like
this one. How the subject has known himself is radically repudiated
in a moment of truth. Doors to its own ruins are thrown open
through the trans—"temporal index" across time to others who may
share its plight (Benjamin, 1968, p. 254). The subject has encountered
the *Real* through the material signifier of her blood, and its bizarre
and terrible gaze. At this instance "one knows that" while Connie is
in serious peril, so too is the subject irrevocably stricken (Lacan,
2006, p. 204).

The traumatic effects of the Lacanian *Real* are made known to the
subject by its utter resistance to symbolization. What I am witnessing is
inarticulatable, unintelligible, and beyond my comprehension. I cannot
separate myself from the material reality of what I perceive, yet the
signifier of her blood would become, what later Lacan refers to as a

master-signifier or "the point of convergence that enables everything that happens in this discourse to be situated" (Lacan, 1993, p. 268). The signifier of her blood incarnates itself into the subject's body making itself known through *anxiety* (Lacan, 2014, p. 88). Anxiety, for Lacan, is a "signal of the Real" and emerges when separation is in question, but separation from what? (Lacan, 2014, p. 207). The effects of anxiety open a space that demands a relating of something to something else.[5] One is required to hold sway and garner a strength to not resist the burden of such a relation. Only then does one know that one has been claimed enigmatically (Lacan, 2006, p. 204).

Vulgar repulsion, horror, vertigo, and shreds of shame take form in the subject, thrusting it into another dimension of time that cannot be incorporated into a teleological narrative. We cannot shake it, as Anne Caron reminds us, because "Shame lives on the eyelids" (Critchley, Bennetts & Tutt, 2014, p. 8).[6] Shame greets us at the mouth of the void that is opening. The subject is radically faced with a fundamental lack, a *nothing* that is irreducible to the signifier that itself cannot be signified except through the effects of anxiety (Lacan, 2014, p. 134). Their own lack, a psychical *emptying-out* or *nothing-ness* engulfs them. In my personal situation, for example, I wanted to vomit and imagined my own body simultaneously evacuating all of its bodily fluids from their various orifices…a gripping memory.[7] The subject bears witness to fragments of a truth about its own existence because it now stands both "*inside and outside* of [*its*] *own* picture," no longer entirely bound to a hegemonic discourse that was in- stantaneously shattered by the sight of Connie's blood (Žižek, 2006, p. 17). In other words, the radical negativity of the void inherent in the subject's core that is experienced somatically in the present cat- astrophe serves as a vector between the subject and its world. It is here that the ethical dimension or possibility for subjectification opens up with the constitutive madness and disorientation that ensue.

Lacan, in a later work, would designate *objet petit a* as the object cause of desire from which the "sharp goad of the enigma" is pro- duced (Laplanche, 2014, p. 96). From this perspective, *objet a* is *both* the gap (that radical core of negativity) and whatever comes to fill that gaping void in our symbolic reality (Žižek, 2008, p. 178). On the origins of *objet petit a* Lacan (2006, p. 198) states:

The child, in his relation to the mother, a relation constituted in analysis not by his vital dependence on her, but by his dependence on her love, that is to say, by the desire for her desire, identifies himself with the imaginary object of this desire insofar as the mother symbolizes it.

Lacan locates the subject at the centre of his psychoanalytic gaze (unlike American psychologists who focus on ego formation) where it is primordially alienated from its own history and formed within and through its relationship to the impossibility of its mother's desire. The unconscious is not viewed as something "inside" the person, in contrast to Jung's problematic but more as an intersubjective space between people. Thus, the tiny subject is cast (castrated) into an external symbolic network of language as desire and connection are created through language. *Objet a* is not really an object at all, or a person or material reality, but a transferential placeholder for the birth caregiver, the *one I hopelessly seek in the other*. As such, *objet a* can never be obtained and as such animates the drives to seek what is lacking from my life (Lacan, 1981, pp. 76–78).

Connie's arresting predicament penetrated a void in each of us that in turn *singularly* inaugurated transferential fantasies directed toward *objet a* ("what does she want of me?") that in turn produced the production of the master signifier. Meaning, for the Lacanian subject is sought through a signifying chain of language in and through its relationship to iterative loss and the impossibility of a unified psychic life. The master (signifier) is empty, however, and not part of a chain of signifiers because it is self-referential and only gestures to itself.[8] That is, no narrative about Connie's blood can provide relief about what is happening here, and so a psychical remainder hangs in the still air like raw sewage that none of us can escape. The Real of Connie's blood is *shared by all of us* and therefore becomes a hegemonic "nodal point" around which our overwhelming libidinal excess would collectively organize (Butler, 2014, p. 190). In other words, in spite of our differences, our incompatible identifications, values and life experiences, the shared enigma, or empty signifier, of Connie's blood can "only function as an *objet petit-a*" (Hook & Vanheule, 2016, p. 8).

Gripped with dawning *intuition* that there is something he *does not know* that exceeds the factual evidence, the subject reflexively turns outside himself for the key (Lacan, 2006, p. 205). He turns to the broader social field of psychical intersubjectivity to verify his existence (ibid, p. 206). This turn to a social field to find itself is a fiction generated to tourniquet the haemorrhaging of its impossible desire for reunification generated from the Real of Connie's blood.[9] Meaning, according to Lacan, can only be created as part of a signifying chain of language through encountering the real of the Other itself, rather than narrativized through egoic accounts of reality. Nevertheless, phenomenological consciousness is at this point completely unaware of *objet a,* being caught up in its own phantasmatic longings to regain its moorings within its tribe. "Are others claimed as well?" "If so, what is my place in the face of this predicament?"

The second moment of structural time, that of subject in relation to intersubjectivity

Lacan identifies the second structural moment as *"the time for comprehending"* what was *seen* in the *"instance of the glance"* (Lacan, 2006, p. 205). The subject finds itself reflexively positioned in what Lacan refers to as the imaginal realm where questions regarding *who* and *what* I imagine myself to be in relation to you and others are generated. My *fantasy* of who I am to you in a given community forms the very coordinates of my identity, sense of belonging and existential purpose (Hook, 2008, p. 279; Lacan, 1981, p. 235). Intersubjective engagements shape my narrative about what is important to believe, whom I identify with and what I must do (rules, customs, practices) in order to be a part of things.

The subject of this second moment is distinguished through his bafflement, doubt, continued anxiety, and curiosity about what is happening in relation to his social milieu. The imaginary ego is captured by a net of signifiers contained within a socio-symbolic field (Lacan's symbolic order) through which the identity of any term (or key signifier) is determined by the historical structures that the subject has itself not created. The subject struggling for identity stands in-between the tension of recognition of others and for an identity whose frame of reference is impossible because of his place in history (Butler, 2004, pp. 150–151). A gay person living with AIDS in the height of the AIDS pandemic is in double social jeopardy. He cannot be recognized by his polity on two counts because the historical structures that determine who is valued in a society and who is worthy of care (or mourning) do not include the gay person, or the person dying of AIDS (Akca, 2017; Butler, 2015).[10]

Lacan is mostly interested in the structural positionings that *underlie the Symbolic order* and the contingency of symbolic values that gravitate toward a *key signifier* because the truth of the subject can only be realized through a crack in its discourse. Discourse "stands in between language and speech" or at the point in which the two intersect and is the starting point of any possible authentic speech (Hoens, 2006, pp. 94–95). However, the subject of our vignette is not yet capable of discourse and instinctually turns toward the imaginary realm of intersubjective identification because he cannot, at this point directly identify with himself (through the haze of his own raw sewage) but only with the image of another that he feels reflects him or at least "what [he] would like to be" (Žižek, 2008, p. 105).

Elsewhere, Lacan would describe the initial actions of the subject into the social field as "egomiming" (Lacan, 1991, p. 180). Egomiming is limited to the subject's perception of others as being "like me." "Who is thinking what *I am thinking?*" "Who is feeling what I am?" phantasmatic communications at this level may happen within a glance. With another dimension of consciousness, the subject is felt capable of role-reversing with the *other* or can imagine that the *other being* is itself an "other" and not just its pure reflection (Lacan, 1991, pp. 180–181). Communications (apperceptions) between group members from this dimension, if we could put pre-theoretical utterances into words, might be symbolically conveyed thus: "What are *you* seeing? "What am I seeing?" "What am *I* to you? " "What do you want of me?" "What do I want from you?" "What is happening?" The constituting subject continually folds back to itself to reflect, cogitate and think abstractly about the weight of these transactions. With mounting anxiety, the subject begins to perceive tentatively a "we," or can situate itself in the place of a "we." "Where do 'I' stand with "all of you?" (Lacan, 2006, p. 207, pp. 211–212). Nevertheless, this tentative perception of a "we" obtained by a constant recourse to the other's desire (who is thought to hold the *answer* to what I am seeking) is still inadequate. Derek Hook (2008,

p. 278) adroitly outlines the futility of these nonreciprocal structural inquiries this way:

> This desire of the subject to locate itself relative to the question of the Other's desire [however] is destined to constant failure…an incessant querying of the Other's desire, assumption of a hypothetical answer gleaned from their gestures and actions; a gradual wearing thin of this hypothesis as inadequate; and then, once again: a renewed querying of the Other's desire.

Thus, the self is internally divided and "hemorraging," as Critchley et al. (2014, p. 7) describes it, "a kind of half-being that is splintered between different kinds of experiences of desire." The subject feels a desire to flee from the wound (a kind of *nachträglich*) that is reflected back in a gaze of Connie's blood, alongside of other contradicting affectivities such as feelings of profound tenderness toward her, oneself, and others (Critchley, 2009).[11] The subject cannot penetrate the key to his mystery, so redoubles to the initial sensorial awareness of Connie's claim in the first structural moment. He dares to wonder with more clarity; "What hold does *her* blood have on me, and the others?" "What am I to *her*?" and "What is *she* to *me*?" and further, "Who is *she* to *them, of which I am one*?"

The fantasy-driven intersubjective transactions of the second moment culminate with the "growing illumination" of a singular truth that has to do with *returning to Connie's impossible claim* sustained in the first moment of logical time encountering *her blood* (Lacan, 2006, p. 168). The psychical hold of the master signifier of her *blood* in other words begins to shift to *the one* who is bleeding. "Maybe, *she* (or what my fantasy of what she is becoming to me) will have the key to what I am not finding here.…Maybe, *she* is the "*one who is supposed to know*" what her blood foretells, for me, or all of us." The time for comprehension concludes when the subject has objectified the very intuition that inaugurated its entrance into the second movement, born of the first that now "blazes a path" into the third (Lacan, 2006, p. 206).

The third moment of time, logical collectivity: we are not only leper-things

In this third moment of time, *who I am* is not only mediated by a second object, but also by a *third,* a third that exceeds the "we," intuited in the closing of the second structural moment. The third is *the other's Other* or *objet petit a,* who is the unconscious remainder of the initial wound that formulated the subject. In other words, the child's mother first occupies the position of big Other and is traumatized through the discovery of her lack, her incompleteness or imperfection. The big Other who timelessly dominates the narrative about what matters in all levels of collective discourse is carefully sutured into significance by fantasies that are generated by our transferential relationships between the image we have of ourselves and the belief that the big Other (*or objet petit a*) is *not lacking.* Our fantasy motivations, to be absurdly simplistic, are constructed to hide *the nothing* that is *the lack* in the Other and *our own primal resonances and resistances to it* (Žižek, 2008, pp. 147–148).[12]

The subject of our narrative now turns to Connie, the third, the *other of the Other* who is the remainder of the object-cause of desire (mother), the Lacanian *objet petit a.* The claim Connie has on me, or rather the symbolic investiture I have in her as an *ego-ideal,* makes itself known through Connie's *lack. Her* lack is symbolized by the void of her womb revealed through the real evacuation of her blood. Her blood reveals her lack. Being must return to the wound of the encounter from which Connie's devastating lack is revealed. Here, the subject must face Connie's impossible demand, *to give her what she lacks* (her lost object), but now it dawns on him that what she lacks is *not his to give.* He is called to give her what *he does not have,* or is *his* to give, one of Lacan's many definitions of love (Lacan, 2006, p. 516). What Connie needs is beyond her own capability to acquire, her own lost object *or* the subject's ability to help her. The full effect of the transference is mobilized when the subject identifies with something that the Other's other is not aware of and more importantly is singularly meant for him to make use of. He cannot save her, heal her from AIDS or put her blood back into her body. Nor, can *he save himself.* He must face the two lacks, his own failure to meet the letter of Connie's impossible demand *and* his own constitutive lack, his own lost object of which he now only has a momentary glimpse. This momentary glimpse reveals an inescapable and singular poignancy, thus ushering the subject from the inter-subjective discourse of the Imaginary realm into the Symbolic. *This movement inaugurates what we are calling trans-subjectivity* through which a collective truth *may become known.*

Let's break this thought down further. The subject's field of psy-chical inquiry has now opened further beyond his discourse with an intersubjective "we" and the egoic guided desires that unfolded in the second movement. The discourse with the other of the Other, directed by his transferences with Connie (*objet a*), now opens him to a new, terrifying and fascinating (*jouissance*) field of desire. The subject is now compelled to face his own *timeless* shame, for *being* impotent and helpless in the first place, for *seeing* Connie in her absolute naked helplessness *and* for turning away with repulsion. "I am ashamed for my repulsion by the sight and smell of your vaginal blood." "I was repulsed looking at your bleeding vagina (yet could not look away) and at the very virus ridden blood that is killing *both of us, no, all of us.*" "I am ashamed for hating myself for having AIDS, for how I contracted the virus in the first place and for turning away from my own raw helplessness."

Suddenly, a new thought flashes up that pivots the subject from the present field of desire to another psychical borderland between *two other* phantasmatic and somatic bodies. "*Was this a birth or death room?*"[13] In such moments, we can feel the powerful recursive pull of the Hegelian *Aufhebung,* where the subject steps backwards with a new rush of anxiety and then goes under into [even] deeper timeless ground, a ground that has been there all along (Giegerich, 2005, pp. 6–7).[14] We can almost hear the psychical churning of *prima materia* where formlessness incarnates itself further seeking its own logical other.

Desire for Lacan is always known through the body (Lacan, 2014, p. 216). The subject can only traverse the libidinal weight of the question so far without going up in flames. However, from this new perspective the subject can *see* Connie and himself with raw and open eyes. This occurrence reveals a new dimension of temporality through which the subject is given a present that is not cut off from a haunted past or future but contains both. The subject "opens up historicity" through the voices of others past and present to which he is now able to respond (Akca, 2017, p. 317).[15]

Another question arises. "What do "*I*" want of *myself* in relation to *your* need?" "What do you need of me that requires *me* to *exceed how you have been cared for* in our world and *how I have cared* or *been cared for?*" And further, in another stunning bolt of clarity... "She relies on *me* to know how to *be* and *what to do* no matter what.*" Hook, through Vanheule and Verhaeghe, gives us a clarifying summary of how the subject is mediated by its ego ideal while engaging the big Other:

> In Lacan's interpretation, ego-ideals are symbolic elements that the subject takes from the discourse of the [O]ther. This means that they are nothing but privileged discursive elements: specific traits and characteristics of others that arrest a subject's attention and are unconsciously adopted to the extent that they are considered to imply an answer to the riddle of the [O]ther's desire.
> (Vanheule & Verhaeghe, 2009, p. 397 in Hook, 2018, p. 132)

A new relationship between a bloodless woman and a mindless man becomes strangely animated by an *objet a* between them that is shared yet not entirely their own. New life flashes up from her bloodless body and is directed to his lifeless mind and back again to hers and so on and on. The subject can now deduce: "H*er* fate is also *mine* and *all of ours.*" The logical reasoning in the third moment opens with the subject's formulation of a truth it now believes is shared by the group.

We see here another iterative manifestation of trans-subjectivity. The singularly invigorated "I" apprehends a new "we" perspective only now perceived from the collision between what is finite in being and what is not. It is here that the subject may begin to translate particularity into some kind of universality, one that levels distinctions between others by recognizing what is common among ourselves as people over time but, at the same time does not disallow what remains irreparably separate (Ruti, 2013). The subject of Lacan's third moment has acknowledged to himself his own limits and culpability in Connie's dilemma and now extends this responsibility to the group through what he believes is a "shared" but yet unspoken truth (Lacan, 2006, pp. 211–212). What the subject has tremulously and still privately concluded may be formally articulated thus:

> *The mortifying effects of shame I feel towards myself for having AIDS in the first place and have likewise inflicted on Connie in her nakedness can now be recognized as not **entirely** originating from my own constituent vulnerability but perpetuated by a brute and senseless reality outside of myself that I complicitly supported. **We are participating victims in a society that condones exclusivity and "we must conceive of ourselves as formally responsible [and] guilty for it"** (Žižek, 2008, p. 247). These societal forces that once gave us a sense of belonging, identity, and hope for a future worth living, have now turned against us when we became infected with HIV/AIDS. The medical system, government and people on the street, even our own friends and family disavow our suffering, treat us like leper-things and look at us with terror and contempt. We have to lie about our health status or else we will lose our jobs, our sexual desirability, our families and friends, our homes or any desirable social standing within the society that we contributed to and depended upon for care. **These norms create the very criteria through which each of us is judged. They are not my own, your own or Connie's.***

The revelation, for which Connie has made her sacrifice, reveals a crucial void within the symbolic order portrayed in an *ideology of carelessness*. From this void and only from it can a new basis of care be created through novel interpretations of what matters, traditions, values, and norms. Nevertheless, the subject continues to doubt why *he* has this mandate and if he is really up to the task (Žižek, 2008, p. 126). When he makes a fundamental choice to act in response to his revelation a new and terrifying space opens to everything through a heightened awareness of lived time. Lacan (2006, p. 212) describes this moment thus:

> Only the slightest disparity need appear in the logical term "others" for it to become clear how much the truth for all depends upon the rigor of each: that truth – if reached by only some – can

engender, if not confirm, error in the others; and, moreover, that if in this race to the truth one is but alone, although not all may get to the truth, still no one can get there but by means of others.

The stakes are high in other words and the subject cannot be certain about what is true or if he is actually serving a shared truth.

Let's return now to the actual vignette where the tendrils of this discussion are rooted. There, I stated that our entire community moved into action, an action born by a *shared rigor.* Whoever initiated the symbolic utterance of truth into action, *"Let's all carry her together to the van,"* is not remembered. The collective gestalt born of a shared revelation whooshed out of us like a baby spinning out of its mother's bloody womb. As Greg Carrigan describes it almost 30 years later: "We could all see our own death then, and it was at the same time so healing because *we were all lifting her on the bloody mattress,* over us, she floated over the top of us." We were, all engulfed in the fierce eddy of unintelligible forces swirling around and through us that somehow, as I believe, Lacan tries to articulate through the culminating movement of collective logic, into a new form of *intelligibility,* a new collective organizing mandate of care. Disease was momentarily elevated from the shame stained status of the leper-thing toward another side of care analogous to love (Critchley et al., 2014, p. 7).

Notes

1 I develop early Heidegger's (2010) depiction of "having become" in relation to the phenomenon of what can also be considered collective individuation and illustration of the Project Quest community at some length (Brooks, 2018 pp. 63–67).
2 Derek Hook masterfully elaborates a theory of the trans-subjective using the illustration of the prisoner's dilemma as Lacan had done in his 1945/2006 essay. He extends his theory from a multi-disciplinary perspective. He is interested in delineating the difference of social psychical theory from Lacan's depiction throughout his collected works attempting to formulate the best aspects of either toward a fresh "extradisciplinary" contribution that has broader applications than either (Hook, 2013, 2018). My focus in this work is to elaborate a psychoanalytic understanding of group phenomena as relevant not only in the formation of the subject but as co-effectively individuating as a response to the effects of real world history, or one's place in history.

3 Daniel Ross explicates Stiegler's critique of Heidegger on this point thus: If politics is the struggle to articulate the *I* with the we, a struggle that requires both the calculation of the future and the incalculability of the very same future, then Heidegger's failure to clearly see that the technical objects of tertiary retention are the basis of every relationship to the future, of whatever kind, proves to be the very reason for his political failure: failing to see the role of technical individuation between psychic individuation and collective individuation" (Ross, 2018, p. 7). Stiegler's primary concern has to do with a massive entropic collapse that renders us into a stupor or a "blind stupidity leading to the madness of those it strips of the feeling of existing—that is, of being themselves worthy of respect, and of understanding themselves as such (Stiegler, 2019, p. 26). Other conceptions akin to crowd stupidity resulting in massive entropic collapse are Heidegger's "They," "*das Man*" or "Inauthentic man" and Jung's "soulless herd animal" (Heidegger, 1927/1962, p. 164; Jung, 1928/1931, paras. 150, 9). See the Introduction to this book for an in-depth discussion of these ideas.

4 Lacan sharpens his distinction between "the little other" or *objet petit a (autre)* and "the big Other" (*Autre*) in 1955 and later (1991, chapter 19). The little other is not really other but an egoic projection activated in the transference (of all kinds) generated within the Imaginary order (see below). Lacan would later flush out his concept of *objet petit a* as the object cause of desire that one seeks through phantasmatic identification's with the other. An important point to emphasis here in light of the *subject* of our essay, is that little *a* transactions are played out through intersubjective identifications through one's bodily affects self-image. Disturbing or immature fixations that are lodged in the fantasies (Imaginary order) may become dislodged through language which is structured in the Symbolic order—the site of Lacan's big Other. Subjective encounters with Big Other-ness messaging are received as radically de-centering because they cannot be assimilated through imaginary identifications (Dylan, 1997, pp. 132–133). The Symbolic order or socio-symbolic field is socially structured by language and cultural laws (codes) that regulate kinship, belonging through ideological messaging. Fantasies (little *a*) that are generated in the Imaginary realm may intersect the socio-symbolic field as the subject struggles with the paradoxes that are evident within a particular ideological situation (big Other messaging) to which one is subjugated. One example is the gay person living with AIDS in a society that does not recognize the value (significance?) of his sexual orientation or respond adequately to the effects of the pandemic (medical care, research, adequate provision for pragmatic or psychological effects on its victims). A contemporary example is the first responder who is authorized by society to treat COVID-19 victims even though they have inadequate protective equipment to do so safely. This subject's struggle to recognize itself as valid amidst societal norms that disavow his value becomes the site of trans-subjective possibilities and collective change (individuation).

5 There are certain resonances to Heidegger's discussions about the ontological difference where *Dasein* finds itself in a middle between being and beings and

what I relay in this sentence (Inwood, 1999, pp. 211–299). See Žižek's *Parallax View* (2006) for another perspective of an ontological gap as the site of subject formation.

6 See Anne Caron: https://kenyonreview.org/kr-online-issue/literary-activism/selections/anne-carson-763879/ <https://kenyonreview.org/kr-online-issue/litera-ry-activism/selections/anne-carson-763879/> Shame is a universal basis of the ethical relation in that it is the affect that accompanies our encounter with an alterity that exposes us to being and the movement of being's possibility. Such a subject is not self-constituting but is given over to the other's alterity, or in Lacan's view, the other of the Other. Shame is the "sharp goad of the enigma," in Laplanche's terms (Laplanche, 2014, p. 96).

7 Julia Kristeva refers to such moments as the "alterity of madness" as "the ground zero of psyche.. spasms and vomit, repulsion, the retching that thrusts me to the side and turns me away from defilement, sewage and muck, a void… improper and unclean" (Kristeva, 1987, p. 160).

8 Stephan Gullatz identifies Jung's reliance on the Self as the empty master signifier through which the terms of Jung's epistemology seamlessly "knots" its meaning into a closed totality (Gullatz, 2010, p. 697). In my view, Gullatz conflates the Jungian master of Self with the World Soul (*Unus Mundus*) as all signification in Jung's problematic comes from and toward it (pointing to itself as unitary source) not the other way around (Brooks, 2011). The collective unconscious is only the World Soul's a-temporal reservoir from which the archetypes emerge as messengers from its unitary source. Giegerich's project attempts to keep his own version of "soul" relevant by intellectually contemporizing it without completely abandoning Jung's vision (Giegerich, 2004). Giegerich is well read not only in continental philosophy (French and German) but also Lacan. He once said that Jungians are "third rate" thinkers while Lacan is first rate (personal conversation, 2008).

9 I am referencing how Lacan's notion of the death drive is activated in the face of ultimate disempowerment by a constant pressure to seek oneness with a primordial lost, displaced or imagined drive object. As I stated it elsewhere: "Think of the death drive as a psychic first responder to a destabilizing crisis whose reflexive and deeply unconscious directive is to turn inward and seek an originary oneness with [*objet petit a*] to avoid annihilation at any cost" (Brooks, 2016, pp. 138–139)

10 See Uljana Akca's erudite and illuminating article titled "Identity as the Difference of Power and the Difference from Being" through which she explores the connection between identity, difference, and power through the intellectual lenses of Butler, Heidegger, and Foucault (Akca, 2017). Ladson Hinton has elsewhere warned us that those who disrupt our illusory ideal of unity (refugees of any kind) are also vulnerable to being culturally scapegoated thus magnifying the "all-too-human tendency to eliminate the troubling other,' whom we blame for disrupting our personal or social worlds" (Hinton, 2011, p. 280).

11 Critchley follows Levinas and Lacan with his own conception of the subject who shapes itself in relation to a demand that it can never meet that divides and sunders itself through the experience of hetero-affectivity. Heteronomy is the determination of the subject in another. See endnote 13 for further discussion on *Nachträglichkeit*.
12 From this point of view, our own blind affiliations to an empty master signifier (as Gullatz claims in footnote 7) can now be seen as a vector to *objet a* and our need to believe this big Other is *not lacking*. Thus, personal wound is connected or transferred to symbolic investments of all kinds.
13 This moment can also be conceived as a Freudian *Nachträglichkeit* or revised Lacanian *Après-Coup* insight in psychoanalytic terms when the here and now trauma opens the patient to an earlier wound. See Brooks, 2016, for a full discussion on this topic and a case illustration.
14 Giegerich actually states; "stepping backwards and going under, rather than a utopian waiting for a resolution." Giegerich strongly veers away from a dialectic that emulates Jung's transcendent function (Giegerich, 2005, p. 7). See also Mills (2002) for an explication of Hegelian sublimation (*Aufhebung*) and its psychoanalytic application.
15 I am correlating aspects of Akca's depiction of Heidegger's moment of *Augenblick* with Lacan's account of collective logic and what I am referring to as a trans-subjective moment.

References

Akca, U. (2017). Identity as the difference of power and the differing from being. *Researching Hermeneutics, Phenomenology and Practical Philosophy*. 10, 1.

Benjamin, W. (1968). *Illuminations Essays and Reflections*. New York: Schocken Books.

Brooks, R. M. (2011). Un-thought out metaphysics in analytical psychology: A critique of Jung's epistemological of basis for psychic reality. *Journal of Analytical Psychology*. 56, 492–513.

Brooks, R. M. (2016). The intergenerational transmission of the catastrophic effects of *Real*-world history expressed through the analytic subject. In *Ethics of Evil Psychoanalytic Investigations*, 137–176, Eds. R. Naso & J. Mills. London: Karnac Books.

Brooks, R. M. (2018). Self as political possibility: Subversive neighbor love and transcendental agency amidst collective blindness. *International Journal of Jungian Studies*. 10, 1, 48–75.

Brooks, R. M. (2019). A critique of C. G. Jung's theoretical basis for selfhood theory vexed by an incorporeal ontology. In *Jung and Philosophy*, 109–137, Ed. J. Mills. London and New York: Routledge.

Butler, J. (2004). *Precarious Life: The Powers of Mourning and Violence.* London and New York: Verso.

Butler, J. (2015). *Frames of War: When Is Life Grievable?* London and New York: Verso.

Butler, R. (2014). *The Žižek Dictionary.* Durham: Acumen.

Critchley, S. (2009). *Infinitely Demanding: Ethics of Commitment, Politics of Resistance.* London and New York: Verso.

Critchley, S., Bennetts, S. R., & Tutt, D. (2014). 'Hamlet's nothing: Berfrois interviews Simon Critchley' retrieved from: https://www.berfrois.com/feed

Giegerich, W. (2004). The end of meaning and the birth of man. *Journal of Jungian Theory and Practice.* 6, I.

Giegerich, W. (2005). *Dialectics & Analytical Psychology: The El Capitan Canyon Seminar.* New Orleans, LA: Spring Journal Books.

Gullatz, S. (2010). Constructing the collective unconscious. *Journal of Analytical Psychology.* 55, 5, 691–721.

Heidegger, M. (1927/1962). *Being and Time* (J. Macquarrie & E. Robinson, Trans.). New York: HarperOne.

Heidegger, M. (2010). *The Phenomenology of Religious Life* (M. Fritch & J. A. Gosetti Ferencei, Trans.). Bloomington, IL: Indiana University Press.

Heidegger, M. (2012). *Contributions to Philosophy (of the Event)* (R. Rojcewicz & D. Vallega-Neu, Trans.). Bloomington, IL: Indiana University Press.

Hinton, L. (2011). *Unus mundus* – Transcendent truth or comforting fiction? Overwhelm and the search for meaning in a fragmented world. *Journal of Analytical Psychology.* 56, 375–396.

Hoens, D. (2006). Towards a new perversions psychoanalysis. In *Reflections on seminar XVII*, Eds. J. Clemens & R. Griggs. Durham and London: Duke University Press.

Hook, D. (2008). Fantasmatic transactions: On the persistence of apartheid ideology. *Subjectivity.* 24, 275–297.

Hook, D. (2013). Towards a Lacanian group psychology: The prisoner's dilemma and the trans-subjective. *Journal for the Theory of Social Behavior.* 43, 2, 115–132.

Hook, D. (2018). *Six Moments in Lacan.* London and New York: Routledge.

Hook, D., & Vanheule, S. (2016). Revisiting the master signifier, or: Mandela and repression. *Frontiers in Psychology.* January 19. https://doi.org/10.3389/fpsyg.2015.02028

Inwood, M. J. (1999). *A Heidegger Dictionary.* Malden, MA: Blackwell Publishers.

Jung, C. G. (1928/1931). The spiritual problem of modern man. *CW.* 10, 74–94.

Kristeva, J. (1987). *Woman Alterity* (M. C. Taylor, Ed.). Chicago and London: University of Chicago Press.

Lacan, J. (1981). *The Seminar of Jacques Lacan, Book XI: The Four Fundamental Concepts of Psychoanalysis.* London: W.W. Norton.

Lacan, J. (1991). *The Seminar of Jacques Lacan, Book II: The Ego in Freud's Theory and in the Technique of Psychoanalysis, 1954–1955* (J. A. Miller, Ed.). New York and London: W. W. Norton.

Lacan, J. (1993). *The Seminar of Jacques Lacan, Book III, The Psychosis, 1955–1956.* New York and London: W.W. Norton.

Lacan, J. (2006). *Écrits: The First Complete Edition in English* (B. Fink, Trans.). New York and London: W. W. Norton.

Lacan, J. (2007). *The Other Side of Psychoanalysis: The Seminar of Jacques Lacan, Book. XVII.* New York and London: W.W. Norton.

Lacan, J. (2014). *Anxiety: The Seminar of Jacques Lacan, Book X* (J. A. Miller, Ed. and A. R. Price, Trans.). Cambridge: Polity Press.

Laplanche, J. (2014). Sublimations and/or inspiration. In *Seductions and Enigmas,* Eds. J. Fletcher & N. Ray. London: Lawrence & Wishart.

Mills, J. (2002). *The Unconscious Abyss: Hegel's Anticipation of Psychoanalysis.* Albany, NY: State University of New York Press.

Ross, D. (2018, May). Care and carelessness in the anthropocene, introduction to a reading of Stiegler and Heidegger. Paper presented at the University of Canterbury, Christchurch.

Ruti, M. (2013, October). The other as the face in post-Levinasian and post-Lacanian ethics. Paper presented at the Psychology & the Other Conference, Cambridge, MA.

Simondon, G (1992). The genesis of the individual. In *Incorporations,* Eds. Jonathan Crary & Sanford Kwinter. New York: Zone.

Stiegler, B. (2019). *The Age of Disruption: Technology and Madness in Computational Capitalism.* Cambridge, UK: Polity Press.

Vanheule, S., & Verhaeghe, P. (2009). Identity through a psychoanalytic looking glass. *Theory and Psychology.* 19, 3, 391–411.

Žižek, S. (2006). *The Parallax View.* Cambridge, MA: MIT Press.

Žižek, S. (2008). *The Sublime Object of Ideology.* London and New York: Verso.

Chapter 3

A subversive reading of Kristeva and sublimation

A subversive reading of Kristeva and sublimation

Since we are open structures, we have our moments of stability – of dependency – that make us invisible. We also have our moments of instability and of opening up to others: to the sun, to the water or to dirt, to the risks that we take.

—Kristeva, 1996, p. 76

Introduction: political possibility through sublimation

In this chapter, I engage the question of trans-subjectivity as it may be conceptualized within psychoanalytic practice. The trans-subjective is posited as a crucial extrapsychical dimension of sublimation and a psyche-social dynamic that is the precursor to social transformation's possibility. I am interested in how this psychical transformation occurs within the individual in relation to others that may open the subject to social responsibility and to ask: What is my responsibility to others, society, the world and to myself? What is my debt to creatures who have no power, voice, or political standing in a world we share? I am interested in how care is awakened through trans-subjectivity in the clinic and beyond (*Sorge*). I am also interested in how creative capacity is maimed, crushed, silenced, and disemboweled by various power structures through which the subject is originally and continually oppressed.

The first section focuses on a critique of Lacanian thinker and psychoanalyst Julia Kristeva's political project inherently built into psychoanalysis (Kristeva, 1996). Whereas Kristeva is reluctant to

DOI: 10.4324/9781003136873-3

extend psychoanalytic theory/practice into the political realm, I elaborate a broader vision of what accounts for trans-subjectivity within a psychoanalysis that today is assaulted by catastrophe. By this, I mean our psyche and body becomes the arena for political contestation and catastrophe's claims (Webster, 2018).

In the remaining sections, I engage what I consider to be crucial theoretical aspects of Kristeva's thought on significance, a rearticulation of Freud's conception of sublimation, that provisionally supports the question of trans-subjectivity in clinical practice. For Kristeva, psychoanalysis enables the patient to more adeptly engage the ferocity of the body's affective semiotic forces (mobilized by drive, desire, and *jouissance*) that animates the subject's movement toward the socio/political realm in the sublimatory process of significance. The extrapsychical or third dimension of significance is also referred to as trans-subjective. From this basis, the subject of psychoanalysis may creatively reconfigure itself and society (trans-subjective) through care (Kristeva, 1996).[1] I posit throughout this book that *trans-subjectivity is the nodal point though which the subject may move from personal concern to political responsiveness.* Because much of Kristeva's thought is grounded in Lacan, I integrate Lacan's thought into the discussion as a means of amplifying or clarifying what Kristeva implies and/or is extending into new theoretical ground in the same manner that I apply and/or extend Kristeva's notion of significance into a broader application. I illuminate the abstraction of theory with the flesh and blood of clinical narrative throughout.

Kristeva's political project: a critique

Kristeva claims the political project built into psychoanalysis is one of permanent revolt inaugurated through separation. Separation is achieved by engaging the negation of identity (lack) and the various power structures by which one is originally and continually oppressed.[2] The political manifestations of intimate revolt may hold sway after the termination of analysis. She personally creatively engages various works of poetry, literature, philosophy, cultural phenomena (feminism, revolutions), and religion (to name a few) through a psychoanalytic lens throughout her works. Because Kristeva theorizes intimate revolt as a political project inherent to psychoanalysis, I question her reluctance to extend psychoanalytic theory into the political realm. On this topic, Todd McGowan reminds us that for Marx, the entire purpose of theory is to facilitate social change and any political project "by its very nature" shares this goal (McGowan, 2013). He links Freud to Marx through social antagonism seen by both to be the root of suffering manifesting in class struggle for Marx and psychical suffering for Freud. He further claims that Kristeva's position puts psychoanalysis at odds with Marx's emphasis on the centrality of praxis, or rather the centrality of facilitating social change in response to the full arch of *social* antagonism (due to the effects of capitalism) (McGowan, 2013). While Kristeva would not claim to be a Marxist, she certainly referred to Marxist theory intermittently in her works from which I will highlight two salient points in departure from McGowan's observations.

Kristeva finds a kinship with Marx's "immanent method" (or praxis) as it played out in class struggle through work and production *and* her semiotic method that plays out in psychical suffering in the individual. She claims that Freud's notion of work (*working through* dreams) goes farther than Marx's structures of work and production could. By this, I suggest she means that semiotics precedes Marx's actual categories of production because working through symbolic formations of the mind is pre-productive (preceding language or thought) (Kristeva, 1986). Second, she also identifies implications of Marx's insight into the crucial importance of praxis (imminent method) *for* semiotics (Boer, 2008; Kristeva, 1986). Marx's historical materialism or theory of history and subsequent economic analysis of capitalism overturned what was known as economics by means of critiquing economics from within the limits of its theory.[3] Kristeva claims that the semiotic method also critiques itself through a continual process of self-questioning provoked by psychical antagonism (loss) through which the speaking subject is iteratively organized, elaborated, and constituted.

While Kristeva actually states that psychoanalysis can bring intellectual ideas (theory) and practical solutions (praxis) together that may lead to social transformation, she does not consider social transformation to be an immediate agenda of psychoanalysis (Kristeva, 1996). On the other hand, drawing on her actual experiences living in

Bulgaria during the demise of the "Marxist social experiment," she states: "Now one realizes that one cannot just make the system of a society from the model of ideology. *It is necessary to transform it.* But not on the side of it, but by passing to the other side" (Kristeva, 1996, emphasis mine). In this statement, Kristeva is in alignment with Marx who throughout his works maintained that social reformation had to occur within the full course of capitalism before something novel could arise through collective struggle. While claiming that *social change must occur from within a (particular) system of society*, Kristeva is also implying that *the individual has a place in social transformation but only when one begins from the collective, not outside of it.*[4] She is making two points. First, a new society cannot be transformed by an outside ideology. New thought and/or reform is informed through a shared struggle from within the system—Marx's point and Stiegler's. Second, social transformation begins with the *semiotic struggle* of the *individual* among others who share a distress and work through it together (Kristeva's contribution to Marx's first point). In other words, Kristeva *appears* to be suggesting, and I am in full alignment with my reading of her here, that trans-subjectivity (sublimation) occurs when the subject exceeds itself in a co-effective relation to the collective (other) culminating in social change. Otherwise stated, we can only have a sublimatory relationship with ourselves when we are co-engaged outside of ourselves and, in this case with others, beyond the analytic frame. This second point requires further elaboration as to the role of community in subject formation.

Through a secular reading of Pauline doctrine, Kristeva somewhat clarifies the role of individual psychic distress and its relationship to how a community may be transformed through a people with whom this distress is co-effectively shared (Kristeva, 1991).[5] As an aside, Kristeva's interest in turning to Pauline doctrine for historical reference to revolutionary dynamics relevant to our present epoch of catastrophe (or so I call it) is shared by other psychoanalytic thinkers and/or philosophers such as Badiou, Jung, Žižek, and Heidegger whose thought I engage in Chapter One. Kristeva lauds Paul's conception of *Ecclesia,* or ecclesiastical community, that was comprised of a plurality of foreigner's (impossible unity of strangers) whose collective agency arose from *non-human* sources. These non-human sources are implied to be the extrapsychical, co-effected dimension of a "we" that enhances the individual's capacity to navigate the on-going tensions between various structural domains in community life such as—self and social, psychic, and other than psychical, drive and desire, imaginary realm and symbolic and so on that I describe in later sections below. Kristeva does not emphasize how shared cata-strophic conditions (diaspora, despotism, plague, systemic racism) may activate a trans-subjective element in early Christian revolu-tionary community, although it is implied.

Trans-subjective agency from this perspective (catastrophe) be-comes accessible co-effectively with others who also recognize a shared dependency that divides them within themselves (Kristeva, 1991). Endorsing what is referred to as third-wave feminism, she does not choose difference over identity (or vice versa) but instead theo-retically explores multiple identities (within such a society) including multiple sexual identities within the formation of the subject. We find in Kristeva's notion of trans-subjective agency—a third extra-psychical dimension of sublimation—a kinship with Homi Bhabba's (1994) third space of enunciation. It is within the third space that Bhabba argues a hybrid cultural identity arises through "the in-scription and articulation of culture's hybridity" (Lu, 2020, p. 19).[6] Kristeva, Bhabba and Lu are making distinct arguments for the hybrid nature of both subject formation (gender, racial, psychical fluidity) and culture itself. In other words, it is through our differ-ences that we may find a common ground through a universal pre-carity of our bodies revealed to us in a shared crises. In such moments, we may begin to translate particularity into some kind of universality, one that levels distinction between others by recognizing what is common among ourselves as peoples over time but does not disallow what remains irreparably separate (Brooks, 2016).

Along these lines we find certain resonances with Judith Butler's notion of the universality of human precarity due the vulnerability of our bodies and fundamental dependency we have on each other. These vulnerabilities are made known to us through the fact of our psychological and biological dependencies, the risk of losing these attachments and subsequent risk of psychological and/or physical violence to us because of this exposure (Butler, 2006). Kristeva ela-borates further on the effects of such a shared dependency:

Tearing oneself away from flesh to heart, from despondency to enthusiasm constituted a true transubstantiation, which Augustine precisely called a pilgrimage. Transforming the foreigner into a pilgrim did not, of course, solve his social and legal problems. But he found, in Christianity's *civitas peregrina*, both a psychic momentum and a community of mutual assistance that seemed like the only solution to his uprooting, with neither rejection nor national assimilation, the religious element preserving the ethnic origin, which it dominated at the same time through the availability of a psychic and social experience that is other. (Kristeva, 1991, pp. 83)

Kristeva implies that trans-subjectivity (semiotics, sublimation... "the tearing oneself away from flesh to heart") is the extrapsychical agency ("momentum") behind a form of collective egalitarian caring that *is socially reformative* without regress to dissolving the "I" with the "we" (national assimilation) (Kristeva, 1996). While improving on what is missing in Marx (the *semiotic shared struggle of individuals* among others), Kristeva does not allow Marx to improve what is missing in her theory of semiotics. What she *does not theorize* is the relationship of the "I" with the "we" (others) outside of the analytic cauldron and how in the face of collective catastrophe, the "we" may be sublimated into social reform. This process is what I have defined as the political in psychoanalysis elaborated in the Introduction of this book.

Kristeva does not go far enough, in my view. While her depiction of sublimation (as will be seen) brilliantly describes the many psychical and extrapsychical processes within the analytic couple her euro-centric, and dare I say *bourgeois*, psychoanalytic insularity, does not imagine into the collective manifestations of trans-subjectivity (Chapter Two) and/or how these effects may manifest within psychoanalytic practice.[7] Whereas Kristeva is reluctant to extend psychoanalytic theory into the political realm, I attempt to do just that within the context of the trans-subjective conceived as the vector through which socio/political structures may be apperceived and potentially engaged within a broader vision of what accounts for psychoanalysis. My basic argument is that the trans-subjective component of sublimation is the necessary link or nodal point through which the subject's *political responsiveness* becomes possible and may be enhanced in the clinic, especially in our current era of sustained emergency (contingency, catastrophe).

The *political,* as you may recall from the introduction *is the struggle* to enunciate the "I" with the "we"—a fruitful collective individuation—*without* dissolving the "I" into the "we"—or regress to collective disindividuation—equated with Heidegger's *Volk* or Jung's "herd animal" (Jung, 1928/1931). That is to say, how we become is always mediated by our socio/political engagements that co-create our social realities against which one may or may not enter a creative political struggle to become. My agenda in developing such a conceptualization of the political has three parts. First, I want to make the case that psychoanalytic perspectives that retain the sovereignty of the analytic couple alone are disregarding how the reals of our social worlds (or sustained emergencies) are inscribed in our mind/bodies every day, deeply effecting each of us. The COVID-19 pandemic is an example of a catastrophe that has inscribed its many psyche/social effects into the bodies of a global community. Allowing for, apprehending and co-engaging the discursive and extradiscursive antagonisms provoked by the effects of such a pandemic in our patients (and ourselves) is crucial if psychoanalysis is to remain relevant.

Second, the existential wound of the world (pandemic, unprecedented climate change, civil rights atrocities, global economic collapse, governmental denial) may open the subject to its constitutive lack (or primal wound) whose fertile dark crescent becomes the very site of subject formation and sublimating possibility. These a*près-coup* encounters with reals of collective catastrophe, such as a pandemic, radically disrupt a coherent sense of reality marked by temporal disruptions and profound disorientation experienced through unbearable bodily intensities such as shock, horror, repulsion, dread, mindlessness, powerlessness, paralysis, and/or anxious waiting to name a few (Brooks, 2016).[8] Last, sustained and unpredictable catastrophe may also activate a sense of urgency to politically respond (in any way small or large) in the face of its impossibility either because our personal lives have been radically disrupted and/or the injustices experienced by others now becomes suddenly untenable.[9]

By extending the political into psychoanalytic theory we may expand not only how we think about what psychoanalysis is but also who may practice it (not just anointed psychoanalysts) and how it may be applied. I give a clinical example below that hovers toward the traditional territory of *"wild psychoanalysis"* in that I was working with individuals who were living and dying of AIDS.[10] My colleagues and I had to think outside of the traditional parameters of what was considered to be psychoanalytically informed therapy and created new ways of working and thinking about what we were doing *in situ*. Further, I was not an ordained analyst yet, neither of us were although we shared an ethos for group practice (see Chapter One). Following Marx, new thought and reform is informed through a shared struggle within the system to which we are all inured. That is to say, we can only have a sublimatory relationship with ourselves when we are co-engaged with others within and beyond the analytic frame. Let us now turn to a reading of Kristeva's notion of significance with a consideration of how she is influenced by Lacanian theory.

Lacan and Kristeva similarities and points-of-departure

Kristeva's post-Lacanian approach is guided by central tenets of a "post-structuralist" engagement with Freud where she among others (late Lacan, Foucault, Derrida, Butler, Deleuze to name a few) would take issue with the structuralist assumption that meaning was a structure versus a process (Kristeva, 1996).[11] Below, I relay a rather lengthy quotation to introduces the conceptual importance of this distinction:

> We believed instead that meaning was a process of heterogeneous logics, a polyphony of representations, a "trial." A "dissemination," an "abjection," and a "horror." In different ways we tried to highlight the heterogeneous, contradictory and multifaceted nature of the psychic apparatus, and thus of human experience itself. Our work produced a conception that broke free from what could properly be termed identificatory thinking. Identificatory thinking accepts the unity of man reduced into his consciousness and so enjoys dissecting human practices into psychological or sociohistorical categories...This new conception unveiled the hidden part of the iceberg, a part that proved to be quite active: a network made up of contradictions, of endless questionings, of

shifts from one level of representation to another...psychotic states, hallucinatory or oneiric [dream] states, sexualities, marginal or rebellious groups—we made passion into the unexpressed side of normalcy. (p. 259)

Meaning, in other words, is singularly conceived in relation to alterity (others) through ever-shifting levels of discursive and "extradiscursive" dimensions of an unfixed and contradictory nature of the human experience.[12] While discourse has more to do with the structure of language systems (symbolic), the "process of heterogeneous logics" on the other hand refers to the extra discursive "polyphony of representations" made known to the analysand within a sublimatory process Kristeva refers to as the semiotic. The semiotic is the affective dimension of language that facilitates an anarchic, diversified, incongruous, and consonant libidinal flow of drive energy. While more primitive than significance, the semiotic constitutes the basis of all imaginative activity intersecting the meaning-making processes of significance facilitated in psychoanalysis. The third extrapsychical "scene" of significance (neither drive nor language) arises through a dynamic springing forth of being enabled by the productive harnessing of these semiotic energies (Kristeva, 2000). From this conceptual overview, we are now positioned to put flesh on the bare bones of Kristeva's basic thesis that I provisionally use to supplement my argument for the trans-subjective as a nodal point for creative engagement.

Kristeva's conception of significance is indebted to Lacan's ontology of the decentered subject who is inter-relationally constituted within a psyche-social dimension *outside itself*. She situates key aspects of Lacan's formulation of the speaking subject (*parlêtre*) into the notion of *significance*. Let's first explore the relationship between Lacan's "subject of the statement" and "subject of enunciation" as backgrounding theory that Kristeva's notion of sublimation both considers and enlarges upon (Lacan, 2006). For Lacan, the subject of the statement refers to how the subject appears to itself and to the other somewhat equated to egoic inter-subjective day-to-day discourse. The subject of enunciation on the other hand is that which emerges from within one's speech through language and may be differentiated from the egoic "I" of the statement. As Lacan stated it "the subject [of enunciation] exists not insofar as it produces discourse but insofar as it is produced, cornered even by discourse (Lacan, 2009). From this statement, we can see that the Lacanian subject is not the agent of its speech as much as it *becomes through the act of speaking within a field of the other* (Lacan, 1999). Through the act of enunciation, the subject has access to unconscious processes through discourse that are situated "in the locus of the Other" (Lacan, 1993, p. 268).[13]

Lacan's Symbolic realm can be characterized as the *symbolic* aspect of language that is rule-governed, logically ordered, and canonized in various ideological discourses through words and other significations instantiated in social and cultural networks we are always, already embedded in and born into. Language for Kristeva is not a static and closed system of signs, but a dynamic symbolic meaning-making process comprised of vocal and corporeally inscribed rhythms described above as semiotics. Both Lacan and Kristeva claim that language production is constantly moving between the Imaginary (the semiotic for Kristeva) and Symbolic realms throughout our lives and requires the subject's ability to contain its imaginative resources in such a way that that the signifier's hegemonic law (Symbolic order) is evaded through the capacity to creatively engage its predominating discourse. Or, to quote Hook who is paraphrasing Hemmings (2005): "the body has the capacity to interrupt social norms, to 'go its own way,' to embarrass the subject in reactions that transgress prevailing discursive values, even though the affective force in question never escapes the broader parameters of the symbolic" (Hook, 2012). The body's *affective force* (mobilized by drive, desire, and *jouissance*) what Kristeva refers to as the semiotic (imagination) animates the subject's movement toward the Symbolic realm and back again in a sublimatory process she calls significance. Creativity, she insists is always a Symbolic enterprise, in the end even though semiotic energies are resourced.

What generates affective force in the first place is the subject's engagement with a destabilizing psychical and/or real-world event that Lacan refers to as the traumatic real. In Lacan's tripartite structure of psychical reality, each realm held equal significance in the business of constituting subjectivity. Lacan positioned the Imaginary (egoic fantasy-unconscious), Symbolic (language and representation), and the traumatic real as knotted together in a living process that informed the singularity of the subject through its traumatic encounters with the traumatisms in everyday life. The real is alterity (pure difference) and violently penetrates the body when encountered. One is viscerally *thrown* in Heideggarian terms as the scene of the real is inarticulatable, unintelligible, and beyond comprehension, therefore outside Symbolic meaning-making possibility. Encounters with the real give us access to our primary process material that may be translated and retranslated within a psychoanalytic process. While Lacan and Kristeva disagree on details (some more important than others) they generally share basic theoretical similarities, making it impossible in my mind to not ground the latter's work in the formers. This introduction to Lacan through Kristeva will serve us well in the last and coming chapter. Let us continue to build in layers of theoretical complexity with as light a touch as possible.

The semiotic, abject, and imaginal (Oedipal) father

Kristeva theorized a crucial distinction between the *"semiotic"* and the *"symbolic"* realm of meaning, a significant departure (or elaboration) from Lacan's conception of the Symbolic register that would establish her originality as a theorist (Kristeva, 1984). Kristeva's semiotic is situated at a point *prior to* Lacan's Imaginary, *preceding* the moment when the infant identifies with its own image, thereby distinguishing "me" from "other" (Kristeva, 1984). The semiotic envisions a chaotic force field within the infant that is anterior to language *(pre-thetic)*, spatially position-less yet provisionally moving through the body that is not yet distinct from the maternal body.

Extending Lacan's notion of the real, Kristeva conceptualizes the abject with the eruption of the real in our lives. Abject as primal repression precedes the establishment of original object relations, desire, representation and a capacity to discern consciousness. As with Lacan, the signal of the real, or abject for Kristeva emerges when separation is in question (Lacan, 2014). The abject marks the moment when the subject recognizes the boundary between "me" and the "[m]other" (Kristeva, 1984). Kristeva argues that this recognition designates the first separation of the child from its mother, a fated recognition that is accompanied by fascination and horror. Most crucially, *the subject does not yet exist* but is in a state of separating from the mother who is not yet an object but a "pseudo-object," also referred to as an "ab-ject" (Kristeva, 2002). It is from this very site (abjection of the maternal) that the "first stranger"—the ab-ject—inscribes itself in the subject so that one becomes a stranger to oneself, a split subject.

How can we understand this striking conceptualization of becoming a stranger to oneself inaugurated by the cleavage of abjection? The abject for Kristeva is foundational to self-formation and marks a zone of repulsion/fascination in each of us in regards to difference (alterity) and how difference triggers the reals of separation throughout our lifetime and trans-historically (1982). We can think of the abject as demarking a departure from the timelessness of merger into experiences of many kinds of temporalities where a past memorial becomes imprinted on psychical memory as a remnant, and future becomes a possibility as the subject leans into the insistence of being. Now, if the subject encounters various forms of additional trauma at this point including more extreme and systemic forms of societal abjection where one *becomes the ab-ject* of another or a society (adoption, bullying, racism, sexism, classism, genocide, etc.), they may emit semiotic traces of non-existence or non-being in the transferential field. The intimate repellent of alterity (strangeness) when repressed may be directed externally by replacing itself in another body, object, or thing, including the analyst. The relationship between what the subject abjects within itself or that which has been psychosocially (and trans-historically) displaced onto one will directly impair one's relationship with one's body, sense of being (identity), intersubjective (egoic) fantasmatic relations, and investment in one's place in a sociopolitical realm. I engage the question of abjection and its psychical promulgations on a societal scale in Chapter Four with regard to reals of race and/or sexual orientation and AIDS in Chapter One.

Signification and language (akin to Lacan's enunciation) for Kristeva may occur only at the advent of the thetic phase at the "threshold of language" (Kristeva, 1984). Kristeva theorizes an original account of a pre-Oedipal period in the imaginary father that facilitates, she argues the infant's original separation between ego and m(other-object), or proto-object (1987b). She views the imaginal father to be the first identification that, in broad brush strokes, makes language, care, and love possible and extended in the subjects extended social relations in the broader world. In other words, it is through the imaginal father (not the m(other) but other becoming) with whom the subject is not separating that new ways of care and being cared for may develop. This is an important point because, through an identification and engagement with a good enough (aka Winnicott), imaginal father (or other caregiver), the subject begins to builds a capacity to self-identify through another loving connection that becomes a bedrock for later expressions of caring about ourselves and others (Winnicott, 1971). This identification with an object outside itself constitutively changes the maternal-fusion-space, thus inaugurating a pre-thetic symbolic capacity within the life of the infant. This space of differentiation (individuation) is supported by the imaginary father who holds open the dynamic structures mediated by various significatory (semiotic) practices driven by a force to detach or isolate the proto-object.

Separating from the mother's body (somatic realm) requires a necessary and violent form of matricide that allows the infant to form loving connections outside of what could otherwise become a suffocating primal bond. To be clear, this is a violent and traumatic scene wrought with contradictory and confusing affective forces (drive energies) whose psychical imprint is immemorial and only detectible in semiotic traces to be translated in the analytic scene. Kristeva follows Lacan here with the idea that, if the mother's only object cause of desire is her child (*object a*), then her child will be tethered to the insanity of being a phallus (or lack) for the mother. The imaginal father hypothesized by Kristeva offers a signifier whose function is to give the child access to intersubjective symbolic reality that exceeds the narcissistic fantasy of the child as said sole object cause of the mother's desire. Hence, transferring fantasmatic *jouissance* toward a loving imaginal father both disrupts the maternal fusion and empowers new psychical experience premised by a distinction between internal and external and subject and "other." While the traumatizing effects of "[murdering] the soma" in order to "transform" a body are irrefutable, Kristeva claims that such a necessary loss is the tax that "gifts" the subject with itself so that language may be navigated (Kristeva, 1987b).

Clinical applications[14]

The semiotic is the affective dimension of language that facilitates an anarchic, heterogenous libidinal flow of drive energy. While more primitive than *significance,* a semiotic process participates within the signifying practices of *significance* discernable in psychoanalytic practice. How might we detect manifestations of the semiotic within a session? Generally speaking these pre-thematic semiotic significations may be characterized as: rhythmic, disruptive, contradictory, poetic, a-temporal, non-sensical, babbling, silences, instinctual impulse expressions, kinetic activity, or varying affective outbursts. Transitions in semiotic discourse over the course of analysis are highly distinctive and may be characterized as erratic, unstable, and iteratively non-linear. From my own experience, one has the sense of moving in and out of the flow of time with variant temporal sensibilities arising in poly- or monophonic expressions apperceived in the transferential field. These various semiotic temporal qualities may be characterized as accelerations of pace, dead-in-the-water stasis, slow-downs, reversals (regressions), repetitions, lapses of memory, timelessness, sustained or sudden eruptions of anxiety/dread and/or apathy, eruptive forms of humor, break-out profanity (and other libidinal excesses), immutable nostalgia, sudden emerging *après-coupe* events, radical discontinuities, turbulences, contradictions, flow, and breaking through.[15]

The reals of psychoanalysis may violently erupt in a session out of an unintelligible context manifesting in semiotic remainders including dream contents. I think of the transferential effects of these encounters as "taking a body hit." As analyst, I may be suddenly penetrated by a pure body sensation, affect or a radical sense of temporal displacement. The reals of patient trauma are not always simultaneously felt by analyst and analysand but may *somatically open me to the patient's enigma of being through my own.* Otherwise stated, my singular wound is the first responder to the patient's emerging subjectivity—co-mingling transferences evoking ever deepening dimensions of subject to subjectness—the true ground of significance. In this sense, the analyst may hold the transference for m (other) or the imaginal father or both over time. The patient may enter the room already stricken but emptied out by its effects, thus eliciting in me a strange apperception—perhaps a haunting or hovering presence (projective identification) hanging in the air like raw sewage. Or the analysand may talk about a dream or past trauma without apparent emotion leaving me somatically excoriated as if I am caught in a psychical eddy with them from which they are powerless, shapeless and/or oblivious. I (the analyst) may want to vomit of evacuate my bowels, feel the hair on my arms stand up or drop into a cold sweat. I may become swept over with a gravity of inexplicable exhaustion or boredom or alternatively feel overcome with displaced melancholy. I may feel annoyance from a defensive reactivity (the other's, mine, both?) to the patient's way of being or more dangerously non-being. I may sense and/or personally resonate with or defend against what the patient cannot own, such as their violent hate, emptiness, isolation, desire, or be the object of these semiotic forces. In these situations, the patient's access to bodily experience is uncoupled from the mind (or meaning-making possibility) and may manifest in the absence of libidinal investment in one's life or alternatively an over libidinal investment in a life that is not one's own.

I will give you a brief clinical example. G entered my office with bloody and battered feet. He was a mountaineer and had just returned from a traumatic climb as yet unknown to me. Prior to this event, G had only been able to identify a generalized sense of anxiety and was otherwise a stranger to his body except through random sexual hook-ups. G was HIV positive in the early years of that plague when having an AIDS diagnosis was a certain death sentence.[16] His disease symptoms and the effects of primitive treatments in the early days of the plague would throw him into ever-deepening anxiety with what that forbode. Would he live through the winter? Was this his last summer? Mountaineering gave him a sense that he was still alive, vital, and close to the best part of planet earth—above the tree line. He often mountaineered alone, maybe he mused, because gay men did not generally "do" mountain sports. He hobbled to the couch wearing flip flops. The sight of his bloody bandages pulled me into the realm of the real that he was not occupying. I was shocked and stricken by his weeping wounds and wanted to both impulsively stare at his feet and also look away in revulsion. I resisted asking "what happened to you?" waiting to see what would unfold. Silence. He sat in the familiar stance of pondering (*jouissance*) how to begin: "What am I doing here?" "What can you do for me?" and so on until he then fell into another familiar loop expressing his chronic dissatisfaction (*jouissance*) about various others in his fading social orb who perpetually left him feeling unsatisfied and empty. After a while, he broke off and was silent. The silence this time can be described by the absence of ego-other boundaries or borders rendering somatic experience as inchoate, amorphous, and non-demarcated. I recall imagining a dark cloud coming toward me and then enveloping me, suffocating me with foreboding.

In the space between words, I was suddenly moved to walk across the room, which I did and knelt beside his broken feet on the floor. I then gently held each foot, one at a time noticing with my peripheral vision that he was looking at me aghast. I felt to stay kneeling on the floor while lightly holding his bandaged toes and after a while, who knows how long, he broke into soft and strangled tears—at first whimpering, holding back, and then sobbing in a full throated messy, snotty kind of way known to all of us. Holding his toes, I imagined the ice cave opening at the mouth of Emmons Glacier on Mount Rainier where the White River began and how it flowed down the mountain floor to the sea. He had never cried in my office before. When he stopped weeping, I quietly returned to my chair and he then told me the horrific story of the near death experience on the mountain during a solo climb from which he had just returned. He softly spoke in stops, starts, silences, more weeping, reaching for words, inaudible babbling, and rocking his body while holding himself tightly as he squeezed out a non-linear poesis (enunciation).[17] I surmise that when I did not abject his wounded body, G could (himself) occupy a truth about his wounds that allowed him to weep (grieve) and later describe the horror of the mountain accident to someone who could receive his address. We could say the prior force of *jouissance* found a new production of speech through an ice cave that opened and allowed him to grieve (such a deep river) that produced (at least for this moment) a new stance to *jouissance*.

Instead of focusing *only* the *après-coup* event that opened him to the primal scene of the ab-ject (or of abjection), I also wanted to keep in mind how G's sociopolitical placement may also be disrupted or repressively anchored when encountering the reals of his life—such as near-death experience and living with AIDS where he is abjected on two counts—for being a gay man and as leper thing. Our psyches and bodies are the arena for political contestation and catastrophe's claims. A central point of such an analysis has to do with tracking how *jouissance* and/or other bodily experiences (including symptom) may also be grounded in socio-political contexts and trans-subjective possibility.[18] What were his symptoms also revealing about that which was obscured in the socio/political realm? In other words, I considered how G's psychical structures (situated in history) were co-effected by his socio/political placement in society as a gay man living with AIDS in a world that rejected both. I return to this vignette below.

Significance and the trans-subjective

Like Freud and Lacan who retrace the singular genesis of psychic pain through speech, Kristeva encourages the analysand to put into words (conscious) what is unformed (unconscious) via a back and forth reweaving of sense and troubling senselessness (Kristeva, 2002). The semiotic intuitively resists the discord (a dissent and protest) of engaging the Symbolic order revealing traces of the original split (somatic body and mind, the scene of the abject) as indicated in the case illustration above. Body and mind are always inextricably imbricated in language both impelling and pulling apart the logic of its heterogeneous, contradictory, and multifaceted organizations revealing the dynamism of subject's structures over time. Recall the discussion above regarding the hybridity of self (subject) through which culture manifests and vice versa. Through its dislocating movements the subject of psychoanalysis is encouraged to develop and reconfigure, translate, and retranslate the interplay of desire, drives, and *jouissance* in the tensions between body and imaginal ego, imaginal ego and intersubjective, and trans-subjective possibility. The field of significance, in other words is where subjectivity springs forth within the duel co-engaging subjectivities of the analyst and analysand and secondly within the act of speaking within this field where what is unthought *becomes* thought. In this sense, we can understand what Lacan (and Kristeva through him) is referring to when he states that the subject is an *effect of* language (Lacan, 2006).

   For Kristeva, the locus of sublimatory discourse is a horizon of being *outside of the psychical* she identifies as "extrapsychical" or "*trans-*

subjective" (Kristeva, 2000). She uses the term "trans-subjective" more in passing as an adjective describing a dimension of *significance* rather than as a concept in and of itself. She portrays the extrapsychical, or trans-subjective as a third horizon of being that adjoins the imaginary/ drive/unconsciousness *and* Symbolic/meaning-making fields of discourse below:

> The field of discourse—and interpretation—can be understood as a narration nourished by sensations/mnemic traces transposed into narrative signs that are invested themselves; the human being is a speaking being inhabited by Eros-Thanatos and by a third component that is neither language nor drive but overdetermines both: signifiance. The two scenes of conscious and unconscious adjoin a third: extra-psychical. There is a horizon of being outside the psychical where human subjectivity is inscribed without being reduced, where psychical life is exceeded by signifiance. (Kristeva, 2000, p. 59)

The trans-subjective dimension of significance, we are told, complexly shapes and is being shaped by language and drive but is outside of the psychical. The "third" scene of significance (neither language nor drive) arises through a dynamic springing forth of the *insistence of being* and the productive harnessing of these semiotic energies (Kristeva, 2000). As will be seen more vividly in Chapters Two and Four, a more expansive notion of egoic identity is explored that becomes transformed and differentiated through trans-subjective enunciations (following Bhabha and Lacan) with others when encountering the real of a shared catastrophe. Echoes of this idea of collective transcendental agency may also be found in early Heidegger's notion of "having become," argued in his secular contemplation of Pauline doctrine that I discuss further in Chapter One (Heidegger, 2010). Having become is a horizon of being that extends the conception of authentic knowledge of the individual into the communal realm, thus decentering being within a field of others. I describe the extrapsychical phenomena as a co-effective expression of the facticity of being thus uniting thought with others in what Heidegger described as a "unity of a diversity" that occurs within groups under certain conditions toward a shared goal in catastrophic conditions (Heidegger, 2010, p. 64). Having become is a kind of *a priori* extrapsychical openness (although Heidegger would not use these terms) and meaning-giving dimension of existence that I posit enables trans-subjectivity as a co-affected facticity in the psycho-analytic practice (individual and group) and within subversive grass roots enterprises. With this theoretical overview of significance behind us, we may now wade into the deeper waters of desire, the drives and *jouissance*, with an eye toward how each may manifest and be reworked toward a trans-subjective possibility.

The depressive void, desire, the drives, and the illicit jolt of jouissance

Below, Kristeva recounts the centrality of the "depressive void," that is a remnant of the abject (or *lack* in Lacanian terms) and therefore crucial for our understanding the various dynamics of sublimation (1987a). The traumatic real of the depressive void becomes the fertile crescent from which the subject's psychic agency is constituted. Kristeva elaborates:

> Sublimation's dynamics, by summoning up primary processes and idealization, weaves a *hypersign* around and with the depressive void. This is *allegory* as lavishness of that which *no longer is*, but which regains for myself a higher meaning because I am able to remake nothingness, better than it was and within an unchanging harmony here and now and forever, for the sake of someone else. Artifice, as sublime meaning for and on behalf of the underlying, implicit nonbeing, replaces the ephemera....Sublimation alone withstands death.[19]

Symbolization (enunciation) becomes the result of the subject's intrepid attempts to tend to the archaic wound of object loss ("depressive void") by creating a new "object" composed within the field of the other in the analyst who holds the projective transference of its archaic remnant (the ab-ject—the stand in for the original caregiver). We need to burrow further into what is involved here if we are to grasp the significance of Kristeva's scandalous claim that *sublimation (alone) may withstand death.*

The subject encounters the real of a traumatic event that in turn opens it to the archaic wound of object loss (Lacanian lack, Kristevian abject) that in turn animates desire (in relation to the other that I'll get to below) that structures the drives and *jouissance* expressions (Lacan, 2006, p. 168). How effectively we sublimate is dependent on how desire structures itself in relation to what the subject imagines the other wants. Psychoanalysis gives the subject a place to begin to ask the question of their own desire within the field of what the subject imagines the analyst wants of them, the analyst becoming the projective object cause of the patient's desire (Lacan's *object a*) (Lacan, 2006, p. 198). Analysis reopens the symptomatic points in the body in which desire is differentially articulated, shaped, and re-awakened through its various object causes that animate it within the transference traditionally, and I add, within the reals of world catastrophe. This requires a rigorous, tedious, and slow process of discovering how the subject's desire structures the drives and *jouissance* by uncovering how desire is operating in the realm of fantasy (dream and symptom), within inter-subjective relationships, and I add, the socio/political realm. As an aside, while Jung is interested in tracing the psychical traces of soul, or self in the imago realm of dream, image (archetypes) and active imagination, Lacan is more interested in discovering how the subject's desire is organized through drive expressions manifesting in not only the imaginary realm but in the socio/political realm, a crucial distinction I make in the introduction.

When the drives (*Eros*-life or and *Thanatos*-death) become animated by desire's archaic remnant, they reach, out particularly the death drive and reflexively direct the subject to seek oneness with the lost, displaced of imagined object (Lacanian *das Ding*, Kristevian "Thing") (Kristeva, 1987a).[20] Think of the death drive as a psychic first responder to a destabilizing crises or catastrophe of any proportion whose reflexive and deeply unconscious directive is to turn inward and seek an originary oneness with my lost other and avoid annihilation at any cost (Brooks, 2016). The irony is that this movement toward the reflexive fantasy of merger for safety and permanence is actually a movement *against life*. Such a psychical stasis is based on a primitive fantasy of what *was lost* that actually *wasn't*.

Let's delve further into this puzzling paradox. In Lacanian terms, nothing was in reality lost because no such object existed in the first place, only a pre-thematic fantasy—thus forming the basis of con-stitutive lack or the Kristevian ab-ject apperceived as a depressive void. As Ruti amply states it: "Subjectivity in this sense is constituted around an existential abyss that separates desire from fulfillment in ways that perpetuate the subject's inexhaustible [fantasmatic] pursuit of what it perceives as lost" (Ruti, 2006, pp. 118–119). In other words, there is a basic split (abyss, void) in all of us where on one side is the fantasy of somatic union and on the other is symbolic meaning-making possibility accessed through language and world of alterity. The repetitious desire to break through the pleasure principle (that limits or bars satisfaction) to ground itself through a form of sa-tisfying unification with the (imagined) lost Thing is death drive driven by jouissance (Lacan, 1997). The drives, in other words, define the trajectory of its jouissance. The paradoxical result of transgres-sing the Symbolic limits imposed by the pleasure principle is not just pleasure but what becomes painful pleasure if not domesticated (analyzed) (Lacan, 1997). The very existence of such a prohibition creates a desire to rigorously transgress the limits that cover the lack to which the subject has been exposed by a traumatic real.

Desire and drive are inextricably related in that the object of desire is also that of the drive (Lacan, 2018). Now it must also be said that even though desire and drive want the same Thing, drive is always closer to the visceral real of the body and historically linked to the particular desire of the historic Other (lost object). Desire is stimu-lated when the drive engages any form of social prohibition where a big Other blocks the subject from its access to *jouissance*. A good example of big Other prohibition that has evoked *jouissance* re-sistance can be found in the social restrictions such as sheltering in place and mask wearing imposed by various governments to prevent the spread of the COVID-19 virus. One way we may interpret some of the responses that negate the science behind these safety measures (*I* am safe, the virus is only like the flu, science is not real, God will save us) is that these rationalizations are productions of unmediated death-driven *jouissance*. Or put another way, the basic needs of the subject to survive (biological instinct) *wars against* the basic needs (desire) of the body for equilibrium and merger (with the imaginal Thing) to such a degree that death-driven *jouissance* overagitates the subject and directs it to ignore the social prohibition (purview of the pleasure principle) in spite of possible deadly consequences. What or who the Thing is imagined to be defines our singularity through our ongoing relationship to desire and what obstructs it throughout life. Psychoanalysis is a means of arbitrating this process (bearing the fierce tension of the semiotic drives via sublimation) as a way alleviating our foundational helplessness in relation to the ongoing encounters with the traumatic real without going up in flames (Ruti, 2012).

When *jouissance* erupts, there may be found a third in every fantasmatic dialogue—a hovering interlocuter, the Thing to which the subject's *jouissance* is directed (Lacan, 1993, pp. 76–78). This hovering interlocuter is the ab-ject for Kristeva—the Symbolic big Other that is a substitute for originary lost object, Lacan's object *petite a*. For Kristeva, abject *jouissance* expressions are heterogeneously organized around the subject's response to the real of the original pre-linguistic breakdown between any distinction with itself and the other *and* itself and the world. Therefore, what is abject cannot manifest directly as a *desire for an object* because the subject does not know it and therefore cannot desire it (Kristeva, 1982). The wound (of separating with caregiver) prefigures meaning-making structures associated with consciousness, language, and the Symbolic order. In such an absence, the subject designates a phobic object in its place as a substitute for the subject's abject relation to the drive. On this Kristeva states: "The phobic object shows up at the place of the non-objectal states of drive and assumes all the mishaps of drive as disappointed desires or as desires diverted from their objects" (Kristeva, p. 35). We see in this statement a desire that is constitutively structured by a force of *jouissance* that is ambivalent toward the object it reaches for while rejecting it.

Let us catch our breath with a very brief and *hypothetical* example of death-driven *jouissance*. In other words, this a compilation of what I have read or heard about and/or imagined into for our purposes. A single man sheltering alone at home during the COVID-19 pandemic and who had a narcissistic rejecting father and impotent mother, takes excessive health risks (to self and others) by participating in online dating contacts that turned into actual hook-ups with minimum precautionary practices. Imagine a well-educated person who believes in evidenced-based science and in many other social realms conducts himself with a sense of integrity. We cannot simply and reductionistically cast him into an anti-science, or anti-humanitarian category. Instead, we may be humbled by under-standing the ferocity of death drive to join forces with a *jouissance* illicit mandate to couple *at any cost*. He is a person who is ex-asperated by the oppressive weight of life threatening anxiety and isolation that is superseded by an unconscious desire to merge with a substitute lost object (phobic object) that never existed in the first place. This is done under the dark of night with others with whom he shares a compatible *jouissance* driven dynamic that instantiates the rules of their game by transgressing societal COVID-19 precau-tionary measures. Herein lies another characterizing quality of *jouissance* (in the neurotic subject) and that is its contradictory ex-pression to what the subject would like to think about himself. The subject in this hypothetical case believes he is "being safe" but at the same time keeps his obsessional dating activities a secret from his family and friend circle. In other words the ways in which we *enjoy* runs counter to our identification, beliefs and ideals ascribed to by Symbolic affiliations and how we present ourselves to others in order to belong. Therefore, how we "enjoy" is often linked to shame, guilt, repulsion, and embarrassment and is typically not a serious topic of dinner party conversation unless we are "enjoying" with others whose *jouissance* instantiations are akin to ours (think of drinking buddies, workaholics, extreme-sports enthusiasts, and so on).

By now it becomes apparent that bearing the tensions of the drives requires that subjectivity does not attempt to overcome its lack but instead resists and inverts abusive dominating injunctions by creating novel responses to it without going up in flames. In other words, the analysand is asked to work with or turn toward the trace wound of constitutional lack that is aggravated by a traumatic encounter of any sort—animating desire and the drive—in order to seek novel life-giving forms of compensation—"to remake nothingness better than it was." Such a vicious exposure to one's own ignorance (via the empty thing and one's resonating deprivation) may also reveal a momentary glimpse into another dimension (the transcendental or what Heidegger refers to as authentic or primordial time) of what it means to be fundamentally human if one can bear the shame, humility, and profound disorientation (Heidegger, 2010).

Kristeva and Lacan saw the area in-between the self (subject, being) and the other as the domain where mental life developed. Signification, or the trans-subjective (extrapsychical) dimension of being, for Kristeva becomes the nodal point through which singularity may find creative expression but not without having productively grappled the ferocity of the drives that constitute the basis of all imaginative activity and entrance into a fruitful engagement with one's social world.[21] But how can we understand the ethical imperative to create something from nothing *for the sake of another* out of the void of the patient's nothing within analytic practice?

Clinical vignettes

In order to ground the abstraction of theory within clinical reality, I return to the vignette about the wounded mountaineer named G. to explicate a point in the analysis from which trans-subjective possibility became the impetus for social change animated by the subject's reflection on his debt to a society that rejected him. Recall, we were living in the early years of the AIDS plague where those who were living with AIDS were societal leper things and there was as yet little governmental or medical/evidenced-based practices to support the overwhelming economic, psychological, or physical needs of those who were HIV positive. G would occasionally attend group events including therapy retreats of the newly forming subversive mind/body clinic I discuss in Chapters Three and Four. I facilitated these retreats with my colleagues. G resisted intimacy through the course of his therapy because of the many betrayals and disappointments he had sustained, including his father's abandonment of the family at an early age, his mother's (single parent) absence holding down three jobs, and what he called gay culture that was not founded on intimacy except through anonymous sex. He had surrendered to his fate, he said but ambivalently continued to come to his sessions. For a while, I was an ideal good mother object interspersed with radical bouts of distrust or criticisms about my failures as a person or as a professional. "What do you know about my life as a gay man, living on a big house on a hill with a child and a minivan? What do you know about AIDS?" I cannot relay the details of these many exchanges due to space and its impossibility given that case narratives are largely fictions, one-sided and objectifications of the patient for the analyst's aims. G's ambivalence about being there, I would say, was a key *jouissance*contradiction—seeking care, comfort, and understanding on one hand while loudly discrediting my viability as a trustworthy person throughout our time together. Desire was split between a half-ruined hope for a loving relationship and predominant terror that this desire would lead him to full ruin, could kill him and maybe it was killing him already given his AIDS diagnosis. Had he been looking for love in all of the wrong places (if love even existed) and was that why he had become infected in the first place?

In one particular session, G was challenging my knowledge about the latest medication his doctor had given him, a person whom he liked because he felt she was a straight shooter and spent extra time discussing with him the latest research on HIV disease because she saw in him an affinity for medicine (a derivative good mother or father identification). They were becoming friends and he was invited to talk on medical panels she was organizing to inform the public about AIDS through his voice. In Kristeva's terms, his doctor was no longer an ab-ject on whom he projected his fear but in Lacanian terms an *object a*, the object cause of desire with whom he could construct companionship and mutual aid over an immemorial depressive void whose spectral presence constantly hovered in the shadow of corporeal death. The Doctor was now the ideal *object a,* and with me he could work through his death driven *jouissance* ambivalences through the flaws of my being and my capacity bore its ferocity, and woundedness.

In this particular session, after describing the valor of his Doctor, he suddenly barked: "You don't know anything about AIDS and what it is like." He said it with such malice that I shivered and am certain that the blood drained out of my face. His face was fixed in a mask of hateful distrust (the no-Thing) in contrast to the sublime Thing of his Doctor. There was no in-between place for a flesh and blood relationship with G most of the time. In his crushing gaze I managed to have the thought that he was inscribing a kind of deadly venom into my body through my own wounds. By this I mean the wound of my own abjection vibrated in resonance with his. I managed to look bravely into his hateful half-ruined face and say something like this: "I don't know what it's like to live in your body, to give myself shots regularly just to live, to wonder if every day will be my last, if any man will want me or of if I will ever be able to climb again." His face remained rigid holding me in his abject gaze. Then, I said something like this: "I think you are letting me know what it feels like to be an object of loathing, a leper...alone and afraid and uncertain." My lips were trembling, but I could now feel my own life force rising in me as he had touched me intimately somehow, and I believed he knew it. I had shown him my underbelly just as he had shown me his.

We were both silent for a long time. He looked down and I was suddenly released from one libidinally charged state now falling, falling into another choreographed by the goad of his enigma and my own. I was shaken. What was his claim on me that I was so viscerally effected? And then I knew that through him I was also speaking to myself, to a terrible sense of isolation that arose unbidden or rather in response to his suffering to a truth of my own. He looked up and I met his glance. New life flashed up from a half ruined heart directed to my own and back again in this extrapsychical space between us, from which the logical reasoning of the moment opened G with a formulation of a truth he now could sense was not his alone, but shared. A new relationship between a heartless man and a clueless woman had become strangely animated by an *object a*—a remaking of something out of nothing that between us is shared but not entirely our own. "Robin," he said, his voice and body trembling, "I have been thinking about this for a while...will you help me organize a climbing group for people living with AIDS?...You are better with groups, and I need your help....If you help me organize, I will teach you how to go above tree line."

It must be clear by now that I am taking certain liberties by departing from the edges of Kristeva's theory and certainly traditional psychoanalysis and am heading toward my own thesis of trans-subjectivity. Like the original object (m(other) the analyst is also another, a not me, separate from what the patient is now able to grasp is a "me." Like the subject, the analyst can be now seen for their vulnerability (or lack) as a separate being—we are two subjects and not a whole (one archaic somatic body). From the void that opens *between us*—(and within each of us)—a strangely animated new thought *arises.* What is revealed to the subject is that in spite of the differences between the subject and the analyst there is a "we" now apperceived as having a shared fate within a differentiated humanity. From this perspective we can grasp how creating something for the "sake of someone else" is informed through knowledge of the subject's authentic desire, born by engaging the real of one's depressive void that allows the subject to, with open eyes see a truth about the Other's humanity (in this case the analyst's) through which a certain kinship can be born (without swallowing either), from which responsibility to a larger purpose (others who are living with AIDS) may creatively be advanced (trans-subjectively). Our shared but differentiated humanity becomes the creative impetus to remake from nothingness something new (a new object) that benefits us both but more crucially in this case—those who are living with life threatening illnesses. G could move from a space of lonely desolation into a new realm of belonging based on how he was changing in the care he was now giving his own life. Caring about his own life because he had been cared for now (The Doctor, his therapist, the Quest community) allowed him to care about the lives of others in his community who also were living and suffering with AIDS, and for me, an outlier. It was from this basis that G could move into the trans-subjective dimension of apperceiving not only that he had something to offer Project Quest (something from no-thing) but that he had a *responsibility* to share it (for the sake of another). Even though he held a certain death sentence, he could live fully now with others. Sublimation withstands psychical and/or corporeal death.

I want to return to the topic of how the trans-subjective may emerge in a subversive psychoanalysis during the present COVID-19 pandemic and it's intersectional traumas. This is an extraordinary period in world history in that we are collectively experiencing a multiplicity of inextricably bound catastrophes (pandemic, crises of civility, racisms, massive governmental failure, economic downturn, effects of poverty, etc.) that are operationally pinging off of each other and amplifying their various off-gassing reals whose effects are filtering through all creatures and things. The practice of psychoanalysis is/must become the radicalized arena through which we may arbitrate these extraordinary effects through sublimation as a way of alleviating foundational helplessness evoked by sustained real-world traumas with our patients and ourselves. My clinical frame (like so many others) within our era of COVID-19 has been radically

changed. I am now coupling with technology as Simondon anticipated over 50 years ago (1965). I do not, however, find that these
frame inconveniences have negatively affected the effervescence of
transference or how I work with it except that I listen more intently
for après-coup derivatives or rather how the wound of the world is
opening the patient to political possibility through encounters with
their own lack (depressive void).

I will close with two brief clinical examples illustrating the trans-
subjective outcomes that manifested during the intensity of COVID-
19 period of analysis. F is a physician who belonged to a medical
complex (beginning with medical school) that had trained and delivered him into the impossibility of practicing medicine within the
ethical oath he had taken. He knew he was a seasoned and gifted
physician, often working with very complex medical cases that il-
luded others. He also knew that other health care workers felt simi-
larly as he did and that he was not alone in the sense of powerlessness
against the rising tide of the commodification of medicine in his
community. F began to have regular conversations with others in his
community who also felt as he did, often finding himself to be one of
the most articulate about the real of the disempowerment he and his
colleagues were experiencing within a shared fate. He sent me a link
to various resources and organizations within the physician community that validated his and his health care community's experiences in what was framed as "moral injury." Moral injury occurs
when physicians routinely experience the personal and collective loss
of being able to deliver the patient care they have been trained to
provide, and their powerlessness in being able to do anything about it
against the institutional edifice that perpetuates it (Talbot &
Dean, 2020).

One day, F showed me a tattoo symbol he had carefully designed
that featured a fist (black power symbol) holding a stethoscope that
would soon become etched on his body. Shortly thereafter, he
decided to take a leading role in establishing a union for health care
workers with other organizations in the area. Eventually, he was
asked to leave the clinic indirectly because of his subversive union
organizing activities but anticipating this had already applied to
university for a graduate degree in public health policy. He wanted to
be a part of the solution in health care reform, not just its victim. F

wanted to have more time at home to raise his children in the short-term and support his wife's career. He did not know where these actions would lead him careerwise, but he wanted to be more fully utilized. He was certain, however, that the health care system was broken and that his archaic desire to talk the lost object into validating his existence was no longer commensurate with how he wanted to direct his creative energies and considerable expertise.

Another patient whom I will refer to as Q is a single parent and computer engineer who had been struggling with a life-long depression (void) whose repercussions manifested in a five-year long writer's block. She is the female child of an emigrant family who fled from a patriarchal society whose traditional cultural practices and beliefs were held by members of her parent's community and nation state for generations. After several years of analysis, the real of COVID-19 served as an antagonizing psychical blow that accelerated the tempo of working through arising semiotic forces that paradoxically delimited what had been a death-driven *jouissance of stasis.* The collective political temporality of *anxious waiting* for somebody "out there" in authority (our impotent government, and our potent biological sciences) to creatively manage the global pandemic crises actually jumpstarted an agency that here-to-fore had been dormant. During this time, Q drew a parallel between the oppressive patriarchal but impotent father-figure of Trump and the suppressed potency of Q's mother (science that is disavowed) *and* her own subjective battle to emancipate herself from that deadlocked (depressive void) psychical marriage.[22] In other words, she had been losing a psychical battle to engage in creative life-giving activities against the more domineering death driven forces to secure a safe and successful (but at times mind-numbing) occupation.

One week, Q just began to write early in the mornings with a creative rigor heretofore unknown to her. She had quite suddenly known to extend the story line of an illustrated novella she had produced years ago but was buried in that drawer of other dead-end projects. I asked her recently what was the question she wanted to answer in her novel. She pondered for a moment. She then leaned into the screen and began to speak within a temporality of enunciation, or rather a form of hypnotic truth telling that was gripping. She said something like the following:

What is my debt to my culture as an immigrant and to my parents who sacrificed their entire lives so that I could live here in the land of the free that itself is a myth? I have inculcated my debt to them in ways that wars with the debt I have to myself…What is the debt we have to creatures who have no agency? What do I owe to those who canno t speak for themselves?

Q's illustrated novel is the discursive answer to these questions and as such is trans-subjective. Such a speech rearticulates ideological constraints into a collective truth that identifies the very limits of politics (the political as described above) and thinks beyond those limits. The act of enunciation occurs in our offices (virtual or otherwise) and through the creative productions that occur in the world at large, in this case the novel Q is writing…not for herself (alone) but for the sake of the characters she engages and sublimates throughout—those who cannot speak for themselves, other refugees not yet emancipated from the trans-historical (psyche/social) contracts they too were born into. She writes through the wound of her being that is the arena for political contestation and catastrophe's claims. I have to comment on the synchronicity (in the Jungian sense) of her truth and mine both arising simultaneously within the COVID-19 months unbeknownst to either. I refer to the questions I posed in the opening paragraph of this chapter that bear a striking resemblance to those she posed although different lenses. In other words, we co-effect each other when we engage from a subject to subject dimension that opens to trans-subjective cross pollination or a kind of psychical hybridity that allows for a differentiated humanity to co-exist with and for each other in mutually fruitful exchanges.

The following chapter engages aspects of Lacan's early thinking on "collective logic" where the trans-subjective is inaugurated by encountering the reals of a particular shared catastrophe with others (Lacan, 2006). I develop my thesis through a study of (post) slavery racism in the United States today illustrated by Killer Mike's speech delivered at the Mayor's Press Conference in Atlanta Georgia on May 29, 2020, sparked by George Floyd's killing by a Minneapolis police officer.

Notes

1 Kristeva thus describes the analysand as a "subject-in-process" who "submits to social conventions [of the Symbolic realm] but does not entirely submit" thus remaining in a constant state of tension (Kristeva, 1996, p. 26).

2 Kristeva builds her argument on her reading of Freud's sense of the Oedipal revolt and the return to the archaic or an antidote to the threat of lost memory. She reframes three figures of revolt from Freud as follows: (1) revolt as the transgression of a prohibition, (2) revolt as repetition, working-through, working out, (3) revolt as a displacement (Kristeva, 2000, pp. 1–20).

3 The philosophical undertones for Marx's theory of history can be found in his appropriation of the Hegelian usage concept of *Aufhebung* (Avineri, 2019, pp. 18–40). Avineri translated the nuances of this German term employed by Hegel thus: "the internal dialectics of development, when the realization of a concept also leads to its transcendence" (p. 36). Marx uses the dialectical device to actualize philosophy (concepts) by moving from theory to praxis (activity). An oft quoted phrase to emphasize this key Marxist argument is: "The weapon of criticism cannot of course replace the criticism of weapons. Material force has to be overthrown by material force; but theory also becomes a material force when it takes hold of the masses" (found in "Toward a Critique of Hegel's Philosophy of Right: An Introduction" in Avineri, p. 37).

4 See Roland Boer's excellent and unusual chapter entitled "Julia Kristeva, Marx and the singularity of Paul." Boer's critique of Kristeva's sweeping range of commentary utilizing religious text and Marxism is lucid, fair minded, respectful, and delightfully transparent (Boer, 2008, p. 221).

5 I further engage the Pauline subject in Chapter Four illustrated by an auto-ethnographic study I conducted of the early days of the AIDS plague from which a community of care created a clinic for and by the people it served.

6 See Lu's paper "Racial hybridity: Jungian and Post-Jungian perspectives" (2020).

7 Who can afford traditional psychoanalysis (with multiple sessions a week) up against collapsing ineffectual health care coverage, unpredictable global economic conditions perpetuated by a crises of civility and the anthroposcenic collapse that disproportionately effect persons of color? How many people of color flock to our training institutes, author texts or critique the hegemonic discourses dominating our psychoanalytic societies and what are their experiences? See Frantz Fanon's 1952 critique of Eurocentrism of psychoanalysis against his social critique of the psychological harm that colonialism has produced (*Black skin, white masks*). Also see Fanny Brewster's critique of racial discrimination perpetuated in the academic and institutional Jungian community (*Archetypal grief: Slavery's legacy of intergenerational child loss*, 2019). See also Kevin Lu's important 2020 paper entitled "Racial hybridity and psychological liminality: on a father's hopes, fears, and fantasies." Also see Siyat Ulon and Robin McCoy Brook's article "Collective shadows on the sociodrama stage (2018) for an account of a sociodramatic group process that explored the cultural

and psychological biases within a diverse membership attending a Jungian studies conference located in Cape Town, South Africa.

8 According to Jean Laplanche, Lacan reintroduced Freud's term in psychoanalytic literature in 1953 as *après-coup* (afterwardness) (Laplanche, 1999, p. 260). Laplanche examined the broader implications Lacan's interpretation, which recognized both the infant traumatic origins underlying Freud's genesis of the term *and* the relevancy of the immediacy of emerging phenomena in the analysis. He did not conflate Jung's retroactive (preceding from the present to the past) hermeneutic conception with Freud's deterministic conception (preceding from the past to the future) but used both while introducing two other crucial elements that are relevant to my argument that real world historic/catastrophic processes can also make a claim on the subject through *après-coup* phenomena. Brooks (2016) for a full discussion on this point alone.

9 The modern subject, Kristeva argues in *New maladies of the soul,* has lost its capacity to apperceive or represent its experience in imaginatively empowered ways (1995). This "malady" of the contemporary psyche is aggravated by the uncoupling of language (mind) from emotion (body) that makes it impossible to feel passionately about life in ways that it can sensibly manifest. Bernard Stiegler over 20 years later offers a more *urgent* assessment of the wounds of contemporary existence somewhat akin to Kristeva's observation. Stiegler claims that both individuals and *whole societies* (a global sensibility) have lost "the feeling of existing, the loss of the possibility of expressing one's will and [the] correlative loss of all reason for living" (Stiegler, 2019, p. 8). His argument contemporizes Kristeva's concerns for humanity's existential estrangement from the mind (Stiegler, 2019). Stiegler captures our collective stupefying descent into mindless "barbarisms" as a species (Stiegler, 2019, pp. 35–45). One wonders if it is already too late to realistically hope for a creative rehabilitation of critical thought in our present global age of sustained emergency. A closer reading of Stiegler's meta-message however allows us to thread key aspects of Kristeva's mind liberating project through discursive creativity that actually supports Stiegler's more expansive vision of collectively restoring mindfulness and aspiration to the individual *in relation to collective life.* He implores each thinking person to partner with technology that will usher us into a new epoch and facilitate "…the emergence of new forms of thinking [are] translated into religious, spiritual, artistic, scientific, and political movements, manners and styles, new institutions and new social organizations, changes in education, in law, in knowledge or work-knowledge or life knowledge" (Stiegler, 2019, p. 14), as discussed in the Introduction of this book. The golden thread connecting their projects is through what Kristeva refers to indirectly as *trans-subjectivity* and Stiegler conceptualizes as *trans-individuation,* following the thought of philosopher Gerald Simondon (Simondon, 2019).

10 I elaborate on these ideas in Chapters One and Two. Kevin Lu cogently argues that a number of crucial problems arise when Jung's psychology or any form of psychoanalysis is carelessly applied to an understanding of cultural phenomena

without critically engaging different methodological approaches also concerned with these collective processes. He warns us of the dangers of psychological reductionism and essentialism that may occur while engaging in applied psychoanalysis that can mutate into a "wild psychoanalysis" (Lu, 2013). As I discuss in the introduction, my approach can be better described as trans-disciplinary.

11 Kristeva adheres (for the most part) with the general parameters of Lacan's model of psychosexual development, however, she recasts certain valences of Lacan's terms by centralizing the maternal and the feminine in psychosexual development thereby decentralizing Lacan's phallocentric emphasis in subjectivity. In Lacanian theory, a structure concerns the relational nature of the psyche including its inter and intra relational dimensions of self-formation within the field of the other. In later Lacan, we find him moving away from an earlier so called structuralist approach by theorizing a third psychical register of the Real (from this point referred to in lower case as real) a dimension that was lacking from totalizing structuralizing theories. The real could not be structurally captured in language, was outside of intelligibility, random and unpredictable. Neither could the subject (irreducible to symbolic structures), the Symbolic register for which there is always an excess, *jouissance* or the dynamic persistence of the symptom be reduced to complete categories given the heterogeneity of psychical experience. The limited scope of this chapter disallows a rigorous critique of Lacan's structuralist or post-structuralist affinities or the similarities and differences between Lacan and Kristeva.

12 See Derek Hook's (2012) detailed reading of the "extradiscursive" as it applies to racism, especially Chapter Two. Here Hook cites a distinction made by Giddens (1984) on what discursive consciousness is. Giddens states: "Discursive consciousness as the term implies, is made up of those details of my current situation and action that are 'immediately verbalizable,' indeed propositional, which is to say that they are either founded on explicit verbal formulas, or are easily 'speakable,' converted into words," (in Hook, 2012, p. 57). In contrast, Hook's definition of extradiscursive consciousness (building on Habermas, 1998) highlights the following qualities: "pre-ideological (or extradiscursive) ground of comprehension that is never itself discursively thematized but that nevertheless functions as a potent (bodily, libidinal, experiential) means of consolidating ideological values" (Hook, 2012, p. 58). Hook also eloquently elaborates and critiques Kristeva's notion of abjection and the abject (later discussed in this chapter) through a lens of extradiscursivity as conceptually relevant to grasping the psychical aspects of racism that I later refer to in Chapter Four.

13 Lacan makes a distinction between other/Other (*autre/Autre*) or the other, or the big Other. The little is an other who is an ego generated reflection and/or projection, sometimes designated as *a*. The big Other designates alterity, radical difference and as such is an illusory otherness and unassimilable (in the imaginary order) uniqueness mediated by the Symbolic order that mediates subject to other subject relationship. The original Other is the mother and in Kristeva's ontology becomes instantiated when the child is first aware of separation and the

m(Other) object is ab-ject. I discuss abject later in the chapter. For both Lacan and Kristeva, the real of separation is founded on the subject's recognition that there is a lack in the other (we are not One). The mythological mother does not exist, in other words. In what follows, I will capitalize *Symbolic*, *Imaginary* orders and not the *real*. I do this so that Jungians or other psychoanalytic disciplines will not confuse my intended meaning with the word symbolic or symbol and imaginary or image. I describe Lacan's tripart orders throughout this chapter in a layering style avoiding, I hope the formatting of a dictionary.

14 The so called *case illustrations* used in this chapter are a compilation of many clinical moments over time and therefore are fictitious because they are not representing a single individual but many.

15 You will note in Chapter Two a similarity with the temporal distortions found in a clinical setting to Derek Hook's extension of the Imaginary realm as applied to the socio-political situation of racial transition in (post) apartheid South Africa (2012). Also in Chapters Two and Four where I extend a reading of Lacan's 1945 essay on "Logical time" distinguishing a difference "logical" time that is constructed on the basis of what he would later describe as synchronic or timeless structures rather than developmental stages of chronological time. Lacan would further characterize these timeless structures as a pulsating ("temporal pulsation") or opening and closing within the transference (Lacan, 2018).

16 Lacan might characterize her diagnostic structure as that of a neurotic subject noted through the ways in which she expresses herself (speech) and also the way in which the analyst is situated in the transference, in this case in allocating me as a facet of a parent, or that of the big Other (one who is supposed to know) (Nobus, 2000). See Nobus (2000) for a clarifying reading of Lacan's three diagnostic subjective structures and the corresponding forms of jouissance characterized within each.

17 I use this clinical event to highlight a theoretical point only and as stated in endnote 14 represents the shared experiences of a composite of many individuals not just one. I hasten to add that crossing the threshold from no touch to touch is serious clinical business and one that I singularly consider depending on multiple clinical factors. Here is not the space to elaborate on this topic, but in writing—I am inspired to return to it at a later time. See Chapters One and Two for another consideration of touching as healing in a group process.

18 Hook's well-articulated argument regarding an error of emphasis on the real of the body in Kristeva's theory of the abject is this: "This phenomenological array of symptoms (the abject) needs to be read as strictly secondary to the societal force of abjection as a threat, a potential disruption to prevailing norms....ontologically the pre-verbal period cannot be denied—we should be wary of treating what happen here as a means of thinking of later forms of human sociality. After the advent of speech, the imaginary, and symbolic forms of intersubjectivity, there is no return to what went before. It is for this reason that Lacan prefers to think in terms of logical as opposed to temporal sequence, structure rather than developmental precedents" (Hook, 2012, p. 92, footnote 21

and 23). In other words, instead of focusing on the *après-coup* of the abject or of abjection alone, one must *also* keep a keen eye on how the subject's engagement in the Symbolic realm (sociopolitical placement) may be disrupted or repressively anchored. I am in entire agreement with Hook's caution here. A central point of analysis has to do with tracking how desire attaches itself to drive and *jouissance* and/or other bodily experience (symptom) as also a response to sociopolitical contexts and political possibility or otherwise put within an *imminent critique* such is central in Jungian analysis.

19 Kristeva, found in *Black sun: Depression and melancholia*, 1987a.
20 Lacan's and Freud's *"das Ding"* and Kristeva's "Thing" are iterative translations of Kant's borderline concept (noumena or "thing in itself" that Jung also relied on (Kant, 2005).
21 I more fully articulate the theoretical and clinical manifestations of drive theory within sublimation and/or trans-subjectivity as they unfold within analytic contexts including group practice in Chapters One and Two.
22 I am reminded of Germain Greer's comment "Freud is the father of psycho-analysis, it has no mother" (2008, p. 104).

References

Avineri, S. (2019). *Karl Marx: Philosophy and Revolution.* New Haven and London: Yale University Press.

Badiou, A. (2001). *Ethics as Essay on the Understanding of Evil* (P. Hallward, Trans.). London: Verso.

Bhabha, H. K. (1994). *The Location of Culture.* London: Routledge.

Boer, R. (2008). Julia Kristeva, Marx and the singularity of Paul. In *Marxist Feminism Criticism of the Bible*, 204–228, Eds. R. Boer & J. Økland. Sheffield: Sheffield Phoenix Press.

Brewster, F. (2019). *Archetypal Grief: Slavery's Legacy of Intergenerational Child Loss.* London and New York: Routledge Taylor & Francis Group.

Brooks, R. M. (2016). The intergenerational transmission of the cata-strophic effects of real- world history expressed through the analytic subject. In *Ethics of Evil Psychoanalytic Investigations*, 137–176, Eds. R. Naso & J. Mills. London: Karnac Books.

Butler, J. (2006). *Gender Trouble: Feminism and the Subversion of Identity.* New York: Routledge.

Fanon, F. (2008). *Black Skin, White Masks.* New York: Grove Press.

Giddens, A. (1984). *The Constitution of Society.* Berkley: University of California Press.

Greer, G. (2008). *The Female Eunuch.* New York: HarperCollins.

Habermas, J. (1998). *On the Pragmatic Communication.* Cambridge: Polity.

Heidegger, M. (2010). *The Phenomenology of Religious Life*. Bloomington: Indiana University Press.

Hemmings, C. (2005). Invoking affect: Cultural theory and the ontological turn. *Cultural Studies*. 19, 5, 547–567.

Hook, D. (2012). *A Critical Psychology of the Postcolonial: The Mind of Apartheid*. London and New York: Psychology Press, Taylor & Francis Group.

Jung, C. G. (1931). *Collected Works: Volume 10*. London: Routledge.

Kant, I. (2005). *Prolegomena to Any Future Metaphysics*. Cambridge, UK: Cambridge University Press.

Kristeva, J. (2002). *Intimate Revolt: The Powers and Limits of Psychoanalysis*. New York: Columbia University Press.

Kristeva, J. (1982). *Powers of Horror: An Essay on Abjection*. New York: Columbia University Press.

Kristeva, J. (1984). *Revolution in Poetic Language*. New York: Columbia University Press.

Kristeva, J. (1986). *The Kristeva Reader* (R. Moi, Ed.). New York: Columbia University Press.

Kristeva, J. (1987a). *Black Sun: Depression and Melancholia*. New York: Columbia University Press.

Kristeva, J. (1987b). *Tales of Love*. New York: Columbia University Press.

Kristeva, J. (1991). *Stranger to Ourselves*. New York: Columbia University Press.

Kristeva, J. (1995). *New Maladies of the Soul*. New York: Columbia University Press.

Kristeva, J. (1996). *Julia Kristeva Interviews* (R. M. Guberman, Ed.). New York: Columbia University Press.

Kristeva, J. (2000). *The Sense and Non-sense of Revolt: The Powers and Limits of Psychoanalysis: Volume 1*. New York: Columbia University Press.

Lacan, J. (1993). *The Seminar of Jacques Lacan Book II: The Ego in Freud's Theory and in the Technique of Psychoanalysis, 1954–1955* (J. A. Miller, Ed.). New York and London: W. W. Norton.

Lacan, J. (1997). *The Seminar of Jacques Lacan: The Ethics of Psychoanalysis*. New York: W. W. Norton and Company.

Lacan, J. (1999). *The Seminar of Jacques Lacan: On Feminine Sexuality, the Limits of Love and Knowledge* (J. A. Miller, Ed.). New York: W.W. Norton and Company.

Lacan, J. (2006). *Ecrits: The First Completed Edition in English*. New York and London: W. W. Norton.

Lacan, J. (2009). *My Teaching*. London and New York: Verso.

Lacan, J. (2014). *Anxiety: The Seminar of Jacques Lacan, Book X* (J. A. Miller, Ed.). Cambridge: Polity Press.

Lacan, J. (2018). *The Four Fundamental Concepts of Psycho-analysis*. New York: Routledge.

Laplanche, J. (1999). *Essays on Otherness*. New York: Routledge.

Lu, K. (2013). Can individual psychology explain social phenomena? An appraisal of the theory of cultural complexes. *Psychoanalysis, Culture & Society*. 18, 4, 386–404.

Lu, K. (2020). Racial hybridity: Jungian and Post-Jungian perspectives. *International Journal of Jungian Studies*. 12, 11–40.

McGowan, T. (2013). *Enjoying What We Don't Have: The Political Project of Psychoanalysis*. Lincoln and London: University of Nebraska Press.

Nobus, D. (2000). *Jacques Lacan and the Freudian Practice of Psychoanalysis*. London and New York: Routledge.

Ruti, M. (2012). *The Singularity of Being Lacan and the Immortal Within*. New York: Fordham University Press.

Ruti, M. (2006). *Reinventing the Soul: Posthumanist Theory and Psychic Life*. New York: Other Press.

Ross, D. (2018). *Care and Carelessness in the Anthropocene: Introduction to a Reading of Stiegler and Heidegger*. Christchurch: University of Canterbury.

Simondon, G. (October 19, 2019). 'Culture and technics, radical philosophy' retrieved from: http://www.radicalphilosophy.com/article/culture-and-technics-1965

Stiegler, R. (2019). *The Age of Disruption Technology and Madness in Computational Capitalism*. Malden, MA: Polity Press.

Talbot, S. G., & Dean, W. (August 28, 2020). 'STAT' retrieved from: https://www.statnews.com/2019/07/26/moral-injury-burnout-medicine-lessons-learned/

Ulon, S., & Brooks, R. M. (2018). Collective shadows on a sociodrama stage. *International Journal of Jungian Studies*. 10, 3, 221–236.

Webster, J. (2018). *Conversion Disorder: Listening to the Body in Psychoanalysis*. New York: Columbia.

Winnicott, W. (1971). *Playing and Reality*. London: Tavistock Publications Ltd.

Chapter 4

Trans-subjective agency illustrated in the reals of US (post) slavery racism

When black scholars hear the call to equal opportunity in darkness, they must remember that they do not belong in the darkness of an American culture that refuses to move toward the light. They are not meant to be pliant captives and agents of institutions that deny light all over the world. No, they must speak the truth to themselves and to the community and to all who invite them into the new darkness. They must affirm the light, the light movement of their past, the light movement of their people. They must affirm their capacities to move forward toward new alternatives for light in America[1]—Vincent Harding, "Responsibility of the black scholar to community."

In Chapter Three, I claimed that Julia Kristeva's notion of sublimation, particularly the *trans-subjective* dimension of *significance* is co-effected by the reals of socio-symbolic-political experience, without reducing one to the other.[2] That is to say, the world takes hold of the subject through its radical encounters with catastrophe, thus opening what is obscured on the symbolic/political dimension of reality through the psychical apparatus of the individual. From this perspective, the political is conceived as a structural dimension to every human society determining our very ontological condition (Mouffe, 1993). You will recall from the Introduction that in Lacanian theory, a structure concerns the relational nature of the psyche, including its inter- and intrarelational dimensions. Honing in on the psychical dimensions of politicality further, I described the

DOI: 10.4324/9781003136873-4

political (following Stiegler) in the last Introduction as the struggle to enunciate the "I" with the "we"—a fruitful collective individuation— without dissolving the "I" into the "we"—or regress to collective disindividuation. A fruitful individuation is dependent on the structural dimension of the trans-subjective that I described *as the nodal point through which the subject's political responsiveness to the real of a catastrophe becomes possible.*

The political, for Yannis Stavrakakis is seen as the moment in which the organization of social reality takes place through a particular modality of the Lacanian real, that is to say more precisely, when the subject *encounters the real* (Stavrakakis, 1999). His badass-elucidating summary below highlights the centrality of the Lacanian real as the entry point for a political reading on which the question of trans-subjectivity leans and is a demarcation for what is missing in (social) constructivist accounts of political theory:

> The political is not the real *per se* but one of the modalities in which we experience an encounter with the real; it is the dominant shape this encounter takes within the socio-objective level of experience. The moment of the political is the moment made possible by the structural causality of this real, a moment linked to the surfacing of a constitutive lack within our fantasmatic representations of society....It is the moment in which the ontological impossibility of the real affects socio-political reality....it is what makes possible the articulation of new political projects and new social fantasies but is not compatible with them...The political is associated thus with the moment of contingency and undecidability marking the gap between the dislocation of one socio-political identification and the creation of the desire for a new one. (p. 75)

By now we can more clearly see parallels to Kristeva's notion of sublimation within a psychoanalytic frame now linked more decisively to a socio/political scale. Building on Stavrakakis, the real (contingency) opens the gap between what is failing with one socio-political identification that generates desire for a new form of identification through which the trans-subjective may rearticulate ideological constraints leading to collective action and collective individuations. Through Lacan, Stavrakakis links the traumatic *impetus* to create new political projects at a societal scale as a response to the vivifying surfacing of collective lack (deficit) even in the face of its impossibility.[3] Collective social justice movements, such as "Me Too" and "Black Lives Matter" are examples of political activism or movements that arose in radical response to centuries of societal denial of the prevalence of uncontained sexual abuse/subjugation and police brutality, each respectively sparred by singular events that ignited massive collective response.[4]

This chapter's first objective grapples with the question of how we may learn from and ultimately enable critique about how the reals of a particular societal catastrophe may effect both the psyche/social/political levels of experience through a notion of trans-subjectivity—without conflating distinct realities or falling prey to forms of psychologism. To this end, I conduct my study of the trans-subjective through the illustrative lens of *(post) slavery racism* in the United States.[5]

I begin with a cursory socio/historic overview of the revolutionary struggles that maintain and challenge the remediation of racial ascription in the United States today. From this background, I elaborate a notion of *the political time of US racism* in the post-civil rights era and its various collective atemporal indexes. I do not attempt to provide a whole temporal picture of politics but rather to offer vantage points that arise from an ever shape-shifting psyche/social landscape with the aim of illustrating how temporality can be seen as a crucial dimension of psychoanalytic studies. I wish to show how we as political beings might read various *temporal distortions* that express a variety of underlying political complexities, contradictions, and resistances to social change within the context of trans-subjectivity. I am interested in how these temporalities penetrate our bodies, shape our being, negate or invigorate our agency as individuals or within our various collective practices (including psychoanalytic practices) and how we think about what is happening. To this end, I engage Derek Hook's extensive and pioneering psychosocial studies on the temporal structures of (post) apartheid South Africa (Hook, 2013, 2015). I additionally reference Vincent Crapanzano's ethnographic temporal study of late apartheid South African experience of "waiting" perpetuated by white opposition to the equitable distribution of resources and privileges. In Crapanzano's study, it is important to note that both those *who dominated* and those *who were dominated* were distinctly enveloped in the psyche/social experience of protracted temporal delay (Crapanzano, 1985).

Secondly, through a reading of Lacan's essay entitled "Logical time and the assertion of anticipated certainty," I explore how we may articulate the subject's movement through three yet interlocking temporal psychical processes culminating in trans-subjectivity (2006).[6] I follow the movement of the subject to the intersubjective and the intersubjective to the sociopolitical extrapsychical dimension of trans-subjectivity. In order to breath life into theory, I situate a notion of trans-subjectivity within Killer Mike's speech delivered at the Mayor's Press Conference in Atlanta, Georgia, on May 29, 2020. The manifest tragedy that sparked this particular event was the videographed killing of another African American person named George Floyd who was suffocated by a Minneapolis police officers earlier that week.[7]

I now turn to historical/socio context of structural racism in the US from which this study is backgrounded.

Political temporality of US (post) slavery racism

George Floyd's killing invigorated what is being called the largest protest mobilization against militarized police violence against blacks in US history including the civil rights marches in the 1960s. White majority turnout for these protests organized by Black Lives Matters (BLM) and others have far surpassed any other forms of resistance, thus far.[8] The BLM movement was formed in 2017 by three innovative women organizers in the aftermath of Trayvon Martin's murder. As the movement grew, the intersectional dimensions of racial domination, injustice, state violence, and massive incarceration became progressively emphasized.[9] That is to say, by addressing racial domination—other markers of social and embodied differences in which race is lived (such as gender, religion, economic conditions, sexuality, dis/ability) are also brought into the public spotlight. This subversive grassroots enterprise (and others) amplifies the efficacy of Cedric J. Robinson's arguments for leadership that arises within the organic development of the community it serves (horizontally) versus hierarchically (from above or outside) (Robinson, 2016).

There are multiple socio/historic co-factors contributing to widely spread escalating civil unrest and subsequent massive multi-racial social activist responses to sustained racial domination and repression on a global scale. These co-factors include "racial capitalist"[10] agendas further sanctioned by the Trump administration and all levels of government over time, a grossly uncontained and impotently managed COVID-19 pandemic at the national level, the denial of the effects of climate and wider ecological catastrophes, subsequent massive unemployment and displacement in the lower social-economic classes, and spotlight on the health and well-being (access to resources) disparities faced by people of color in stark relief whites, to name a few. "Infrastructural racism" endures and is reproduced even in the broader picture of successful challenges to policy and the ways in which roles and statuses are ascribed (status quo), what Lacan refers to as the Symbolic edifice (Singh, Burc & Soulvis, 2020, pp. 7–8). Think uncritically held police brutalities, unequal access to political representation (voting) healthcare, education, employment, housing, to name a few.[11] The durability and reproducibility of infrastructural determined racisms remains functionally inseparable to our libidinal ensnarement to capitalism (McGowan 2016; Singh et al., 2020, p. 9).[12]

What is at stake here, according to Singh, Burc and Souvlis is the contradictory relationship between the underlying paradigms of national universality and racial particularity with the uncritically held assumption that national universality integrates racial particularities. The American universalism myth, according to Singh, Burc and Souvlis is an expansionist, color-blind discourse that portrays US nationhood as positing open relationships to both territory and population by claiming the virtues of civic openness (fluid emigration policies), religious tolerance, democratic membership in the polity (vote and leadership access), the promise of economic mobility, stability, and religious freedom as outlined in the constitution.

Race and racism remains a "glaring contradiction" to the "American creed of liberty and equality for all" (Singh et al., 2020, p. 7). As Singh, Burc and Souvlis state it… "racial inequality [is] a problem because it threatens American claims to the ideal of world leadership and undermines the idea of America's (exemplary and exceptional) Constitutional democracy [and that America is] the most civilized and secure form of government devised by man (gender stasis)" (p. 8). The myth of

American democracy, world leadership, safety and the promise of civility is conflated with the capitalist driven agenda that remains dependent on processes of racial domination, violence, imperial expansion, colonial dispossession, and genocide. There is growing consensus within scholarly and public debates today that supports the claim that American slavery contributed greatly to modern capitalist economics, what Robinson has termed "slave capitalism" (Clegg, 2020, 2018; Robinson, 2000, pp. 200–203; Singh, 2017; Wolff, 2012). From this perspective, structural racism and capitalism are functionally inseparable and ultimately the resolution of one requires the resolution of both.

While such arguments retain a degree of explanatory force, they fail to consider the psychical implication of racisms generated at least in part by socio/historic understandings. From a Lacanian perspective, we may wonder how the historic commodification of persons into production machinery (things) has enduring (trans-generational) traumatic effects on African America's *sense of being* today. Race from this view is considered to be a fantasy construction generated through white discourse over centuries whose aim was/is to maintain the hegemony of whiteness by projecting *jouissance* (what I lack) onto the racial other (who reifies my lack). Otherwise put, white fantasy objects of race establish whiteness as a hierarchical status by casting other races into *non-being*, what Lacan would call the *master signifier of being* (Fanon, 1952; George, 2016). I return to these important ideas in more detail below.

Singh, Burc, and Souvlis's portrayal of the contradiction between the ruse of American universalism and truth of racial inequality *in addition to* a consideration of how racisms are also psychically instantiated (via *jouissance*) into a given social structure presage the *impossibility* of a society ever fulfilling its utopian constitutional ideals. *I advance the notion that these radical psyche/social asymmetries become the very site of socio-political possibility through trans-individual movements that arise within a committed struggle inaugurated by encounters with traumatic reals of structural racism* (Hook, 2012). Singh, Robinson, and Martin Luther King, Jr., have persuasively argued that the black struggle for social justice for over 400 years has been and continues to be a model of democracy for the nation as a whole within the very specter of impossibility (King, 1991). King reminded us in 1969 (published posthumously) that the radical threshold for a true democracy must be built on an ethos of care (*Sorge*) that indelibly incorporates the needs and aspirations of a differentiated humanity not a fictitious homogenized ideal of unity.[13]

A claim I grapple with throughout this book is that the *very absence (lack) of political mandates of care become the creative impetus* for and by the people most effected by societal abjection that enables the emergence of subversive grass roots enterprises—an argument I deepened in earlier chapters. The emergence of BLM movement is an example of a performative collective individuation—an iterative resurgence of the "black revolution" reanimated by the reverberations of the traumatic real of Trayvon Martin's murder and boldly contradicts the constitutional "fetish" of racial equality.[14] In what follows, I (ambitiously) attempt to extend the present discussion into a broader theoretical consideration of the *socio/political temporality* of US (post) slavery racism within the dimension of *real* time.

The socio/political temporality of US black revolutionary transitional time

In this section, I turn to Hook and Crapanzano's temporal studies of late and (post) apartheid South Africa to expose the reader to an approach that to my mind successfully qualifies the experience of political time for this unique period in history. I consider the applicability of their findings to the present project in an effort to show how we might read the psychical and social experience of (post) slavery racism temporality in relation to the traumatizing and revolutionary flash point of Georgy Floyd's killing.

In Crapanzano and Hook's studies we find a dominating temporal *leitmotif* when encountering the psychical excesses of perpetually sanctioned violence within a society that resists social change—that of *anxious delay* or *waiting* (Crapanzano, 1985; Hook, 2013).[15] Crapanzano's ethnographic study of late apartheid South Africa describes a predominating mode of collective waiting experienced by those who dominate (empowered whites) in opposition to apartheid (1985). However, he soon reminds us that that *both dominated and those who dominate* are equally subjected to the affective/temporal dimension of protracted waiting but the imposing temporal imaginary of each is distinct. Crapanzano elaborates:

For most whites, waiting is compounded by fear; for most blacks, however great their despair, waiting is illuminated by hope, by a belief that time is on their side. For coloured's and asians, there is both fear and hope in waiting. (in Hook 2015, p. 55).

Crapanzano's sweeping characterization of the difference between white collective fear situates the quality of hope on the side of those most oppressed under apartheid (Hook, 2015). For whites, however fear of an imaginable future in which one co-exists with blacks is bound to structural conceptions of race and to the practices of racism (*jouissance* expressions of exclusion, violence, hate, erasure, I add) that traumatically breach the life-giving limits of mind and body for a whole society. Crapanzano does not elaborate how hope is retained in the temporal imaginary of the oppressed class.

Crapanzano further describes the effects of what I am calling *sustained emergency* or living within the delayed real of a particular cultural catastrophe whose outcome is undetermined and beyond the frame of intelligibility. He states:

[I]n the very ordinary act of waiting, particularly waiting in fear, men and women lose what John Keats...called negative capability, the capacity of negating their identity so as to be imaginatively open to the complex and never very certain reality around them...In such circumstances there can be no real recognition of the other—no real appreciation of *his* subjectivity. He becomes at once a menial object to be manipulated and a mythic object to be feared. He cannot be counted in his humanity. (Hook, 2015, pp. 56–57)

Our attention is now drawn to the erosion of the white subject's intersubjective engagement culminating in a diminished capacity for sublimatory agency or what I am referring to as the trans-subjective. Trans-subjectivity is an extrapsychical agency through which the subject's political responsiveness becomes possible and may be imagined forward into collective action. The breaking down of agentic possibility can also be described this way. The "I" fails to individuate because it does not recognize black alterity as being-human. Thus, the "we" on which individuation is dependent through the intersubjectifying function of fantasy (as will be seen below) cannot manifest into a trans-subjectifying possibility. Thus, the field of the black-as-non-being collapses as the white subject regressively implodes into itself into a stasis of fruitless imagination. That is to say, black-as-non-being remains a fantasmatic object of danger (ab-ject) versus a human partner to which I may fruitfully contribute and mutually benefit otherwise known here as trans-subjective possibility. What is stricken from black existence—under the crushing weight of a psychically impotent white gaze (big Other)—are *fantasies of being* from which non-racialized singularities may arise (George, 2016).

Lacan's notion of the "big Other" as a manifestation of the Symbolic order can be defined as a universal structure encompassing the entire field of human existence, action, and experience. It involves, you recall, language and the function of speech that is codified in social conventions, laws and practices that are largely uncritically held unless punctuated by the real. From a Lacanian lens, we may interpret the force of white hate to be generated in the operations of Symbolic realm and felt through the limits placed on social alliances and other over-determined imaginary (fantasy) forms that effect the subject's choices and practices. Crapanzano posits that collective white resistance impairs white individuation because the creative capacity to move into new ways of being in a shared society are truncated. Or rather, the subject's capacity to negate (sublimate or sublate in Hegelian terms) one's identity in order to move into a higher order of thinking and being in response to a new situation is barred. Put in Lacanian terms, the split subject of the dominating white cannot recognize its lack—the source of creative potential — whose cultural and individual modes of *jouissance* (access to pleasure) have long been culturally tied to sadism expressed through forms of violence and subjugation of the other and *put into the other* as non-being (lack) (George, 2016). Lacanian academic Sheldon George underscores how crucial it is for African American's to free themselves from the trans-historic *aphanisic* effect of the signifier of *the slave* in today's moment of history. As Lacan argues, the subject can only emerge as a signifier and is in effect the "slave of [the] discourse" from which one is born (George, 2016). What is curative for the African American, according to George is to "imagine an agency beyond the Symbolic" (George, 2016, p. 19).

What does this imaginal agency entail? George argues that the *African American must not believe in racial identity in the first place* as race is a fantasmatic construction generated by an a-historic white big Other rendering of black being into nothing-ness and a history that is bound to atrocity, becoming the dominating myth that explains one's lack. George posits instead that the African American subject must distinguish between a racially imposed identity (Symbolic lack) and its own subjective lack.[16] I propose that trans-subjectivity *is the necessary agency* that allows the subject and collective to co-effectively separate from big Other aphanisic constrictions on being thus allowing for the possibility of creative and life-giving societal change.

Robinson's critique on the history US black resistive violence concludes that blacks have seldom exercised a level of violence that matched the defiling violence received by dominating whites (2000). Black factical life experience in the Heideggerian sense of things is culturally, collectively, familiarly and ontologically distinct and *grounded in collective resistance.* That is to say, the tendency to turn the effects of real external violence *inward*, according to Robinson is conceptualized as a "renunciation of actual being for historical being; the preservation of the ontological totality granted by a metaphysical system that had never allowed for property in either the physical, philosophical, temporal, legal, social, or psychic senses" (Robinson, 2000, p. 168). This astonishing perspective introduces a trans-historical dimension of abjection within a community whose shared experience of subjugation also harbors a pre-thematic, or semiotic (metaphysical system) potential. This potential grounds black collective resistance (beneath white radar) in a quietly held protective kinship among all of those who produce, share, and exchange a means of survival over time (George, 2016; Robinson, 2016).[17]

Let us return from this discussion to Crapanzano's discourse on the temporal mode of waiting in apartheid South Africa. Crapanzano states further:

Waiting means to be oriented in time in a special way. It is directed toward the future—not an expansive future, however, but a constricted one that closes in on the present. In waiting, the present is always secondary to the future. It is held in expectation...It is a sort of holding action—a lingering. (In extreme forms waiting can lead to paralysis). In waiting, the present loses its focus in the now. The world in its immediacy slips away; it is derealized...It is numb, muted, dead. It's only meaning lies in the future—in the arrival or non-arrival of the object of waiting. (Crapanzano, 1985, p. 45)

Thus, an atemporal quality of anxious waiting is perpetuated by fantasy of what *cannot be imagined* or rather social change and one's place in it with black others. These constricted fantasies may be re-directed instead into many disorganized or fragmented symbolic projections onto something specific such as conspiracy theories, a second Coming, the world coming to an end and so on (Crapanzano).

Hook identifies another form of fantasmatic delay noted in (post) apartheid South African white resistance that redirects anxious waiting not forward but *backwards* in what he terms *nostalgic fixity.* This form of temporal delay not only pushes back the future (that cannot be imagined) but libidinally invests itself on repetitive fantasies of a favorable past that may be distorted by masturbatory (my word), inflationary memories (Hook, 2015). In this scenario, the inability to adequately "fix" or subvert the *time of change* may lend itself to an ambiguous temporality expressed through forms of melancholia by the subject and/or community. On the dimension of melancholia, Hook states:

Melancholia amounts to a seizing up of the time of the living, i.e., that of redeployed or "refreshed" libidinal attachments, the possibility of which is superseded by the glacial time of the un-dead attachment. An ethical gesture can be discerned here; the never letting go of the lost object and the "rehabilitation" of the object within the subject's own maligned ego. (2013, p. 200)

Hook attributes a kind of "un-dead" deadness that permeates a whole collective as relating to a libidinal undead attachment to the lost object on the subjective level that has been sutured into a of a way of life that is giving way on the Symbolic level but cannot be grieved. In other words, the ethical gesture to which Hook refers would require the dominating subject to confront its own lack and ultimately how the white imaginary of race structures its life.

On the heels of this discussion, it is not difficult to apply certain aspects of the political temporality of anxious waiting depicted in the studies of late and (post) apartheid to the distinct political temporality of US white resistance in post-Civil Rights era. We may continue to theorize through George that the *object a* of race (created over time in the white imaginary) sutures over the reals of racism and sustains what Singh has referred to as the myth of American democracy founded on contradictory relationship of national universality and racial particularity (George, 2016; Singh, 2020). There are many forces that have shaped the uneven transformation of post-World War II racial reform in the United States in (what I am now calling) *US black revolutionary transitional time*. For a brief period, the civil rights movement propelled by black demands for reform, critiques by black intellectuals (note the Harding quotation in the chapter heading), activist movements and the movement of many blacks who marched and protested were not entirely ignored (Singh, 2005, p. 13). Singh's cultural–historical analysis describing this period is succinctly summarized below. I have highlighted the temporalities of both white resistance to *and* black revolutionary struggle against such white resistance in *italics* below:

> The *unraveling* of the social and political consensus that enabled the *limited reforms* of the *earlier period* has exposed the *shaky* political, institutional and ideological foundations on which much *racial progress* has been built. The *contemporary reversals of prior movements* toward racial equity reveal *the gains* of the *short* civil rights era as *provisional codifications* of a more complex social reality, *temporary achievements* of *longer-fought* and *still-persisting* social conflicts. More than the *pronouncements* of presidents and the courts, a history of black *subaltern struggle*, *white resistance* and *open and surreptitious racial discord* shaped the *uneven transformations* of post-world War U.S. *racial formation*. (2005, pp. 12–13)

Singh's sobering appraisal encapsulates a temporal index of US black revolutionary transition within the last 60 years of political time and can also be characterized within an arch of the many distortions of anxious waiting described above but within its distinct historical contexts. *Let us remember that the black struggle for social justice has existed for over 400 years and is lived within the democratic struggle to emancipate itself from the hegemony of whiteness towards a mandate of a differentiated humanity.* Contrast this mandate of care with the obscene fiction that perpetuates the structural dimensions of a homogenized ideal of a unified undifferentiated whole against which the black revolution rebels.

US black revolutionary transitional time must be characterized in the broadest of brush strokes as an *ongoing courageous struggle* contained within the specter of impossible hope for an indeterminate future beyond one's lifespan. The struggle for racial justice is an ideal whose aim exceeds one's future but lies with a margin of possibility for a more satisfying manifestation experienced by future generations. From this perspective we may characterize the various temporal distortions that express a variety of underlying complexities, contradictions, and resistances to social change over time as that of protracted anxious waiting. The various temporal indexes we can identify within the rubric of anxious waiting revealed through the reals of US black revolutionary time include the effects of surging libidinal intensities, limited reforms, entropic collapse, collective stupidity, collective disindividuations, incomprehensible interruptions (contingency), nostalgic fixities, sustained emergency, crushing violent setbacks (reversals), provisional codifications, trans-subjective flash point surges, collective individuating actions, temporal paradoxes and contradictions, shaky and disjointed episodic starts and gains, uneven transformations, paralyzing stall outs, political gaslighting, loss of the feeling of existence, dread, and stalled out anxious waiting.[18]

I now turn to an exploration of political temporality through a reading of Lacan's notion of collective logic or what Hook has referred to in other writings as the trans-subjective (2018). Building on George, I consider how the African American subject may imagine an agency beyond the symbolic instantiations of race through trans-subjectivity embedded in a particular temporality of anxious waiting. This study is backgrounded by the reals of George Floyd's public death that ignited a ground swell resurgence of public outcry against police brutality and other racist agendas (voter suppression, COVID-19 treatment disparities, underrepresentation of minorities in government and corporate leadership, etc.) that are now generally considered as one of the many variables contributing to record-breaking black voter turnout in the 2020 national elections.[19] Killer Mike's, also known as Michael Santiago Render, speech is one of many trans-subjective temporal surges delivered at the Mayor's Press Conference in Atlanta, Georgia on May 29, 2020, sparked by the ruthless killing of George Floyd by a Minneapolis police officer earlier that week.

Lacan's notion of collective logic through the lens of Killer Mike's trans-subjective speech

Lacan's 1945 essay gives us a theoretical template through which we may articulate the subject's movement through three distinct yet interlocking temporal psychical processes culminating in trans-subjective possibility, illustrated in excerpts of Render's speech. Lacan illustrates his thesis with the allegory of the prisoner's dilemma where the trans-subjective network (referred to as "collective logic") becomes the basis for consensual reality in relation to a shared dilemma, as explored within a therapy retreat scenario in Chapter Two.[20] I explore how Lacan's temporality may be illustrated through the *interplay of the political time of (post) slavery racism* and *subjective/other experience* elaborated in Lacan's three logical moments. The first moment of logical time is that of the subject who engages the atemporality of the visceral real of racism. The second moment of logical time is the imaginary/fantasy time experienced through intersubjective egoic distortions of anxious waiting. The third moment of logical time is the symbolic time of the social/political forces of racism from which the extrapsychicality of the trans-subjective may rearticulate ideological constraints.

Lacan's first structural moment of time: visceral real of structural racism

We can only imagine how Render was effected in the first moment of encountering the raw truth of Floyd's killing[21] Render gives us an indication in the opening of his speech: " *I know it tore your heart out, and I know it is crippling, and I have nothing positive to say in this moment because I don't want to be here....I am mad as hell...I woke up wanting to see the world burn down yesterday because I am tired of seeing black men die."* When later asked by Stephen Colbert why he had agreed to speak when he clearly didn't want to, Render modestly replied that he was a rapper and could not tell anybody what to do. *"I didn't want to get on the podium because I didn't think I had any-thing to say so I just said what was on my heart."*[22] Robinson describes the historic effects of accumulated brutal degradation perpetuated against blacks in America as profoundly *unexplainable.* Quoting Hobbes he stated "It was not simply a question of outrage or concern for black survival. It was a matter of comprehension" (Robinson, 2000, p. 108). The senses, in other words, cannot comprehend mortifying debasement.

Let us turn to Lacan's first logical gesture that begins the moment the singular subject engages the real of an existing dilemma or "the instance of a glance" (Lacan, 2006, p. 167). The subject is suddenly and unexpectedly wrenched from the banality of everyday "fulgur-ating" time. Viscerally slammed by the collision between contingency of its own temporality and the incontingency of existence—shame, unshakable anxiety, vulgar repulsion and/or horror take hold, and *we cannot shake it.* We are no longer entirely held by the invisible con-straints that bound us into some kind of prior conformity. It is within this state that one may bear witness to fragments of raw truth, the pervasiveness of a terrible reality and our singular relationship to it.

Engaging the real of a natural phenomenon, as Lacan described it penetrates any psychical barriers to the subject's core.[23] Thus, the subject suddenly experiences a psychical emptying out, an evacuating whoosh irreducible to the event that cannot be signified except through the effects of *anxiety.* Anxiety for Lacan is a "signal of the real" (Lacan, 2014, p. 134). "Anxiety is the only affect that does not lie," he insists, while other affects may be subject to displacements, substitutions, or fantasmatic evasions (Lacan, 2014, p. 297). The radical exposure to the void inherent in the subject's core serves as a vector between the subject, its world and world history. Otherwise stated, a truth about the world's wound may open the subject to its own through which one may, with forbearance, intuit something else not yet identified. Herein lies the ethical dimension of the possibility for subjectification and political possibility. The signifier of George Floyd's killing would become, what Lacan in later work refers to as a "master-signifier" or "the point of convergence that enables everything that happens in this discourse to be situated" (Lacan, 1993, p. 268). The subject may now apperceive a larger perspective to the dilemma posed standing both "inside and outside of [its] own picture, no longer bound to a hegemonic discourse that was instantaneously shattered by witnessing the videographed slow and agonizing suffocation of George Floyd (Žižek, 2006, p. 17). Gripped by a generalized anxiety and dawning intuition that there is something s/he does not know that exceeds the factual evidence, the subject turns to the broader field of intersubjectivity for the key (the second moment of logical time).

It is important to note that the Lacanian subject is racially homogenized, or rather, not theoretically particularized to the psyche-social experience of being racialized. Addressing this absence of particularity, Hook describes what he calls the extradiscursive "reals" of black experience exposed to perpetual violence (abjection, humiliation, hate, etc.) as it disrupts the body in relation to the psyche (Hook, 2013). Hook references Fanon's text entitled *Black skin white masks* that over 70 years ago advanced a radical perspective on the effects that white domination has on black identity (Fanon, 1952; Hook, 2013). Fanon describes the traumatic effects of protracted racist objectification in colonized situations through autoethnographic studies he conducted among the black middle class in French Caribbean. His powerful narrativizations of racialized experience are captured through vicerality of living tissue. He states: *"The white man is all around me; up above the sky is tearing at its navel; the earth crunches under my feet and sings white, white. All this whiteness burns me to a cinder"* (1952, p. 94). And still further: *"My body was returned to me spread-eagled, disjointed, redone, draped in mourning on this white winter's day. The Negro is an animal, the Negro is bad, the Negro is wicked, the Negro is ugly; look, a Negro; the Negro is trembling..."* (p. 93). And finally: *"I crawl along. The white gaze, the only valid one, is already dissecting me. I am fixed. Once the microtomes are sharpened, the Whites objectively cut sections of my reality"* (p. 95). Through Fanon, we witness the shattering force of white gaze that tears, crunches, burns, disjoints, negates and cuts into sections the ugly, animalistic body of the other...." remaking black bodily being into its own degraded non-object through the *jouissance* of hate.

We can detect the Fanonian reals of racialized experience in Render's description of George Floyd's killing when he says: *"He [police officer] casually put his knee on a human being's neck for 9 minutes as he died like a zebra in the clutch of a lion's jaw."* From this very "zone of nonbeing," Fanon posits that "genuine new departure can emerge" (1952, p. xii).[24] Let us push further into what is involved here. Recall, the subject in the first moment is gripped by a dawning sense that there is something he does not understand that exceeds the factual evidence (the real of George Floyd's murder) and now turns to the broader field of intersubjectivity for the key.

Lacan's second structural moment, that of subject in relation to others

The subject moves into the second moment of logical time undone by what is unintelligible and propelled to seek an answer to an unformed question gnawing at the outer edges of comprehensibility to which s/he intuitively turns to the Imaginary realm of intersubjective/fantasy ego-identification for an answer.[25] Lacan is most interested in the structural positionings that reverberate from distress revealed in the cracks and fissures of the Symbolic order that are navigated through these inter-subjective fantasmatic egoic transactions that gravitate toward a key (master) signifier. The signifier of George Floyd's killing is incarnated into the subject's body through the truth of an anxiety (that never lies) and what that portends. The truth of the subject can only be realized through a crack in its discourse. Discourse is sublimation from which the structural dimension of trans-subjectivity may arise. Recall from the last chapter, discourse for both Lacan and Kristeva stands in between language (subject of the statement) and speech (enunciation). The subject of the statement refers to how the subject appears to itself and to the other equated to egoic intersubjective day to day discourse—the immediate aim of the second structural moment. The subject of enunciation on the other hand is that which emerges from within one's speech through language or becoming through the act of speaking within the field of the other (Lacan, 1999, p. 188). We are now extending the field of the other from the analytic field of transference to intersubjective fantasmatic exchanges that occur anywhere. The protagonist becomes any of us encountering a shared catastrophe.

At this early point of the second moment, the subject is not yet capable of discourse and instinctually turns toward the Imaginary realm of intersubjective identification because the subjectivity cannot directly identify with itself as a self. Thus the subject turns to making intersubjective appeals to others whom s/he/they imagines will reflect back what s/he/they would like to be (Žižek, 2008, p. 105). These interactions shape my story about what to believe, what I must do to belong, with whom I identify and so on. A lot of what happens within intersubjective activity is unconscious (or barely conscious) fantasy life. My fantasy of who I think I am to you in a given community and the broader world forms the very core of my identity, sense of belonging and existential purpose (Hook, 2018, p. 279). Lacan refers to this early intersubjective discovery as "egomiming" (Lacan, 1991, p. 180). Egomiming is limited to the individual's perceptions of others as being contrasted with one's own. Fantasmatic communications at this level attempt to comprehend ("the time for comprehending") what was seen in the *instance of the glance* in the first moment (Lacan, 2006, p. 205). These rhetorical/pre-theoretical transactions can be illustrated as follows. *"Are you feeling what I am feeling? Who is thinking what I am thinking with regard to the real of George Floyd's killing?" "What is happening here?"*

We have no evidence in Render's speech about his very private and often pre-conscious semiotic utterances. From an after speech interview with Steve Colbert, we do know that Render was not planning on attending the Mayor's press conference that Friday night (Colbert, 2020). He was delivering food from his restaurant with a rapper friend (T. I.) when T.I. received a call from the Mayor's assistant saying that the staged protest that Render supported was turning into a riotous atmosphere, and the Mayor wanted Render to say something at the press conference to help quell any oncoming violence. We only know that Render says he initially did not want to go, and then they both, ultimately, attended the press conference. We know that Render says he was ambivalent about speaking at the press conference. He opens his speech acknowledging this: *"I didn't want to come, and I don't want to be here"*…and later…*"I have nothing positive to say in this moment because I don't want to be here."* Given that we are not privy the structural processes leading to how Render changed his mind, I'll continue with a theoretical accounting of the intersubjective fantasmatic struggle any subject has with the other and how that may advance to the third moment.

Eventually, so sayeth Lacan another intersubjective dimension of communication emerges that allows the subject to essentially role-reverse with another subject now signifying a capacity to see the other as not just a pure reflection of myself but a separate being (a "you," a "not-me") (Lacan, 1991, pp. 180–181). *"What am I to you?" "What do you want of me?"* Eventually the subject can tentatively situate itself in the place of a "we" and begins to reflectively think about the weight of these transactions that pivot to another fantasmatic series of inquiries. *"Where do 'I' stand with 'all of you?'"* (Lacan, 2006, pp. 211–212). At some point after frustrating repetition, it dawns on the subject that what I am seeking cannot be adequately obtained through recourse to the other (intersubjectively) who is thought to hold the answer to what I am intuitively seeking. A lot of social media banter of this sort, for example perpetuates a kind of empty egomiming or vacuous blah blah blah designed to stage or posture oneself that in the end leads to frustration, disappointment and psychical introversion—a turning inward because the subject who is frustrated is yearning for a more authentic engagement that requires turning toward one's vacuous depressive void (or lack) in Kristevian terms.

We must remember (following George), the African American subject's imaginary capacity to differentiate its own subjective lack from Symbolic racialized lack perpetuated by white gaze—interjects another dimension of complexity not accounted for adequately in Lacan's depiction of the second moment of logical time. Affective and/or libidinal intensities may remain in excess of words because these intensities are less amenable to a broader cultural translation. We may think of these formless libidinal intensities as collective traumatic racialized remainders hanging in the air like raw sewage—a particularized potential. The remainder for Lacan is what survives the ordeal of speaking within the field of the other the field of the Other through the presence of the subject, in our case now extended to the psychical traumatisms of racism (Lacan, 1999, p. 188). Therefore, the racialized subject may be acutely challenged in securing a likable self-image because s/he is traumatically tethered to a sort of societal negating fixity that George has argued is linked to the signifier of the slave (non-being) (George, 2016; Hook, 2013, pp. 86–87). The degree to which the subject abjects itself and/or has been Symbolically abjected (racialized *object a* of the slave) will directly impair body image, sense of identity, intersubjective fantasmatic relations (meaning making possibility) and ultimately investment in one's place in a socio/political realm.

Recall from Chapter Three that for Kristeva ab-ject *jouissance* is a *remainder* to the real of the original pre-linguistic breakdown between any distinction with the subject and the m(other) now relocated in the Symbolic realm. Let us burrow further into this thought. The subject's *jouissance* is directed toward the Symbolic big Other that is a substitute for originary loss or *object petite a*—or Kristevian*ab-ject* (Kristeva, 1982, p. 9). The function for *object a*, as Lacan describes throughout his works is not only to signify loss but also to creatively reassociate traumatic loss into the Symbolic realm throughout life (George, 2016, p. 31; Lacan, 2006, p. 198). Signifying loss, therefore becomes an opportunity for the African American subject to redefine identity based on engaging one's own loss at the level of the Imaginary and language, what Kristeva advances as significance or sublimation and I am extending through Lacan as trans-subjectivity.

Following these particularizing and foreshadowing theoretical considerations we may now move to the closure of the second moment. The subject cannot penetrate the mystery that circumnavigates around the initial visceral blow inaugurated in the first structural moment to where the s/he now again returns with great foreboding. It is as if the wound inflicted by the sight of George Floyd vicious killing splinters the subject between contradicting yet vivifying experiences of desire…a visceral repulsion and a kind of unnerving and opening tenderness. The subject then dares to wonder: *"What does he (George Floyd) want of me?" "What hold does his tragedy have on me?" "What am I to him?"* Eventually, a new thought dawns on the subject that requires him/her/ they to role reverse with the group (a collective one belongs to) on this matter. *"Who is he (George Floyd) to them, of which I am one?"*

The second moment of time culminates with the growing awareness of a singular truth that has to do with returning to the subjects fantasy about what George Floyd's impossible claim has *on me* (the "I") sustained in the first moment. *"Maybe he [George Floyd] is the one who is supposed to know what his unspeakable death foretells for me or for all of us."* The "time for comprehension" concludes when the subject has clarified the very intuition that inaugurated its entrance into the second movement born of the first that now "blazes a path" into the third (Lacan, 2006, p. 206).

The third of moment of time, logical collectivity: "Do not burn your own house down!"

In the third moment, *who I am* is not only mediated by the *inter-subjective* transactions with others but also by a third, a hovering third interlocuter that exceeds the "we," the *other's Other,* or *object petite a.* Let's break this down. The other's Other has to do with the subject's primal transferential relation to George Floyd—the remainder that survives the originary division that formulated the subject, its caregiver. The other's Other, or *object a* timelessly dominates the narrative about what matters in all levels of collective discourse and is carefully sutured into significance by fantasies that are generated by our relationships between the image we have of ourselves and the belief that the big Other is *not lacking* (Žižek, 2008, pp. 147–148). This plays out in all of our uncritically held dependencies on institutional authorities of all kinds (my boss, Supreme Court Justices, police officers, the president, my mentor, my parents, my doctor, my analyst, my lover, my priest, my editor, and others who are *supposed to know* or those whose good graces I am dependent upon). Let's turn now to how this these complex unconscious dynamics play out culminating in Render's trans-subjective speech. Until we may directly refer to Render's speech I continue to engage only in a fantasy clinical vignette for the sake of animating the anonymous subject's movement.

The subject of our narrative (any of us) now turns to George Floyd, the fantasy place holder for the other's Other, the third, the object-cause of desire or *object a.* From this point, the subject begins to flush out new dimensions of desire that cannot be grasped in the image of George Floyd's death alone because his death *is the object cause of the subject's desire.* When subject *begins to grok that identifying their own desire is the key to understanding the significance of the ordeal…then the whole process begins to dramatically shift.* The claim

George Floyd has on me has to do with my psychical investiture in him made known through his *lack*. George Floyd's lack is revealed by his powerlessness to make himself be heard. He could not save himself and nobody he appealed to (the police officer, his dead mother, the whole world listening now) responded to his address. His pleas for help fell into a black void of carelessness revealing the poignancy of *his* lack and our own shameful culpability as we too are powerless to act as well. Render reminds us in his speech that while George Floyd was dying under the knee of the officer, he called out to his mother with his dying breath. Render states in his speech *"When a man yells out for his mother in duress and pain, and she's dead, he is essentially yelling, "Please God, don't let it happen to me."* Such unspeakable poignancy. Neither God nor m(Other) intervene, the former is already dead and the latter, well that leaves open the existential question of time immemorial. Where is God? Or bringing the question painfully back home, where were we…where was I?

It suddenly occurs to the subject that *"George Floyd needs me to give him what I do not have and is not mine to give him in the first place."* Giving what I do not have, that is not mine to give is one of Lacan's many definitions of love (Lacan, 2006, p. 516). What George Floyd needs is beyond the subject's capacity to acquire—George Floyd's own lost *object a,* and the subject's capacity to save him from his terrible fate. The subject cannot stop the officer's timeless *jouissance* to crush black life, nor can he/she/they breath air back into the already dead man's lungs. *Nor can he/she/they save themselves* from this kind of ruthless unpredictable violence perpetuated for centuries onto non-white bodies. The subject must now face the two lacks, the failure to meet George Floyd's impossible demand and the truth about its *own* constitutive lack through which it may only have a momentary glimpse. *The subject floods with the momentary flash of a meta truth that its fate is singular but also interconnected with George Floyd's dilemma, as is that of its family, community and society* (Lacan, 2006, pp. 211–212). This revelation inaugurates the *transsubjective* moment from which a collective truth may be known and spoken.

Pushing further into what is involved here, we can say that in a flash, a psychical unbinding (from all kinds of heretofore restrictive norms) reveals a new dimension of temporality where the subject is given a present (now) that is not cut off from a haunted past or a future *worth living*. S/he/they can now hear George Floyd's retro-active dying pleas for help and has the breadth of field to also see oneself, one's family, people and society with raw and opened eyes. Another question suddenly arises. *"What do I want of myself in re-lation to your impossible demand?"* *"What do you need of me that requires me to exceed how you have been cared for and how I have cared or been cared for in this wretched careless world?"* The terrible and enlivening weight of this awareness further penetrates. *"They rely on me to know how to be and what to do no matter what."* The subject can now coherently acknowledge their own limits and culpability in George Floyd's tragedy and extends this responsibility to the com-munity through what they now believe is a "shared" but yet un-spoken truth. *"George Floyd's fate is also mine, and all of ours."*

This private revelation, for which George Floyd has made his terrible sacrifice unveils a crucial void within a social order whose implicit messaging conveys an *ideology of carelessness*. "We *are all vulnerable in a society that condones exclusivity*." From this crack in the social order and *only from it* can a new basis of care be created through novel interpretations of what matters - the instance of Being becoming. The stakes are high however as the subject doubts if they are up to the task and continues to doubt why they have this mandate in the first place (Lacan, 2006, p. 212).

In other words, the enunciation of a shared truth does not mean that everyone spontaneously receives the same revelation and acts on it all at once. More realistically, the enunciation of one's revelation within the field of others becomes the basis for a collective action that is simultaneously shared by enough of the others in various stages of similar (enough) apperceptions. Thus, a thickening gestalt occurs and is acted upon through an extrapsychical tipping point by which others amalgamate and collectively respond to what is now becoming a shared truth.

What makes the moment trans-subjective, or trans-individuating as Simondon poses is the psychical *and* social investiture made by each of us toward a common good (Simondon, 1992). What makes the action *political* Žižek furthers, is each individual's decisive break from a he-gemonic social order whose mandate condones exclusivity (Žižek, 2013, pp. 1–8). What makes the action *psychical* is that each of us must

wrestle with our own structural traumatisms and the fierce antagonisms of death driven (by desire) *jouissance* so that we may define for
ourselves what is real, true and good concerning how we respond to
the dilemma posed by George Floyd's killing and be willing to take
responsibility for our beliefs and actions from that basis.

Let us now turn to Render's speech where the root of this discussion stems.

Killer Mike's speech

Atlanta's mayor Keisha Lance Bottoms invited Render and other
prominent community leaders in the black community to speak to the
rioting youth who were burning parts of the city to the ground at the
Mayor's Press Conference in Atlanta, Georgia, on May 29, 2020. To
my mind, a trans-subjective possibility arose for Render when he
accepted the invitation from Atlanta's mayor to publicly speak to the
rioting youth of Atlanta that *was* realized in the action of his
speaking a collective truth within the constitutive madness and disorientation of centuries of psychical and corporeal erasure. He is
responding to a "moment" (in the history of the civil rights movement in the US) when the value of black life is becoming reframed. So
are the frames through which public grief may be acknowledged and
mourned within a broader social sphere (Butler, 2004). Their shared
heritage is inscribed in the recesses of language, customs, rituals, and
practices that hold their society together as long as they resist the
transmutation of what is sacred by those who hate.

We see on the stage a number of dignitaries, including the Mayor
and Police Chief all wearing masks except for Render who stands in
front scanning his audience. He is trembling. We are his audience any
of us who heard his speech or listened later on social media.[26] The
power of Render's words are conveyed through his raw emotionality,
his humility and his cogent grasp of what was at stake for his city and
the youth who were most vulnerable in this moment of history.

Gasping through tears, Render states that he is the son of an
Atlanta City police officer and has a lot of respect for police officers.
He recounts a history where the original eight black police officers 80
years ago had to dress in a YMCA because the white officers did "*not
want to get dressed with Niggers.*" Several times he states that he

didn't want to come but "I am *responsible and duty-bound to be here….to simply say that it is your duty not to burn your own house down for anger with the enemy. It is your duty to fortify your own house so that you may be a house of refuge times of organization".* Render is speaking specifically to the *"children,"* the young black men and others in Atlanta who in their irreducible aspiration for dignity are paradoxically striking at the heart of their heritage and future out of helpless rage. *"They don't know what else to do,"* Render poignantly concludes.

While Render publicly honors the lives of young black men in Atlanta, Georgia *("I love you and respect you")* he also reminds them that it also *their responsibility, their duty* to continue to build their city in *their own* reflection. He does not condemn their rage but attempts to redirect (sublimate) their misguided *jouissance* toward a kind of revolt that gives human desire its meaning. He invites them to participate in the collective structures already in place in imaginative ways. He gives them context and direction for a purposeful rebellion. *"Plot, plan, strategize, organize, mobilize. We have "a moment now,"* he says, to improve on our failures by supporting the grassroots organizations that are already established and by voting. *"Let's get ahead of it"* Become a *"house of refuge"* for the city that is already ours. After centuries of erasure, he directs them toward the hope for a kind of future they can shape whose basis is the present catastrophe.[27] *"…Will we use this as a moment to say that we will not do what other cities have done? And in fact to get better then we have done? Exercise your political bully power and going to local elections and beating up the politicians that you don't like…Now is your election to do it. It is not time to burn down your own home….Because if we lose Atlanta, what else we got?"*

In other words, the young black man must see how his rioting invests itself in his own oppression as well as the social order that enslaves him. Political subjectivity does not attempt to overcome its lack but instead resists and inverts abusive dominating norms by creating novel responses to it. Revolt in such circumstances seems impossible when one has no power because the values of the land are immeasurably corrupt, and the deck of possibilities is stacked against you from time immemorial. Render calls on the memory of thought and care to those who are closest to Atlanta's black community

(*Sorge*).[28] He calls out to his community from the gap of social negation that *they share*. Render's speech is not the place where political
battles are actually fought. To the contrary, his speech identifies the
very limits of politics—or how culture/society and knowledge are
formulated and *performed*—within the problematic of the particular
situation and thinks beyond those limits into possibilities.

Radical psyche/social asymmetries such as I have depicted above
become the very site of socio-political possibility through trans-
individual movements that rise within a committed struggle inaugurated
by encounters with traumatic reals. As argued in the introduction to this
book, society is constituted through multiple dynamic trans-subjective
assemblages over time into ever evolving social systems.[29] Perhaps we
are now experiencing a surge of *care* and *carefulness* in specific historic
moments within black revolutionary time such as exhibited in Render's
speech, the emergence of BLM, the record black American voter
turnout across the country no matter how one voted. Perhaps we are
building a future against the odds that we—a differentiated humanity
can fall in love with.[30]

Notes

1 In Foreword by Robin D. G. Kelley of Cedric J. Robinson's text *The Making of
the Black Radical Tradition Black Marxism* (2000/1983).
2 Socio-objective politicality speaks to actual governmental institutions policy-
making processes and activities.
3 Stavrakakis does not specifically identify trans-subjectivity as a modality of the
political as I am through my own particularized reading of Lacan's conception of
"collective logic" that I later develop in this chapter. It must also be noted that in
the last two decades other post-Lacanian thinkers have greatly contributed to the
sociopolitical discourse including Alain Badiou, Slavoj Zizek, Derek Hook,
Sheldon George, and Todd McGowan to name a few.
4 Jamieson Webster (2018) is a Lacanian Analyst and scholar who wrote
"Conversion Disorder: The Body as Revolt."
5 Fanny Brewster's focus on "the racism of slavery" contributed to my formulating
the term "(Post) slavery racism" instead of "institutionalized racism" that itself
has become somewhat of a meme (Brewster, 2019, p. 29).
6 In other works, Lacan uses the term "transindividual" that is conceptually inter-
changeable with what in this essay he referred to as "Collective Logic." Hook
renamed the concept "trans-subjectivity, a term that I have adopted (Hook, 2018).
7 Lacan's notion of "collective logic" or the collective expression of a shared universal truth has certain resonances with Gerard Simondon's notion of

transindividuality particularly the supposition that the human subject is both constituting and constituted by objective reality and not the psychical realm alone. Simondon's unique problematic envisioned a genealogy of individuations through which individuals within different orders of complexity (i.e., physical, technical, biological, physical, collective, trans-individual) uniquely engaged the milieus from which their singularities arose. For Simondon, transindividuality of one allows for other individuals to communicate at the level of pre-individual (akin to the Lacanian subject of Jungian Self) thus making it possible for entry into new collective individuations (Simondon, 1992, pp. 307, 310–311).

8 BLM movement is not entirely responsible for organizing all of the protests surging the country in 2020, but the organization has been on the ground providing infrastructural support for many. See: New York Times article "Black Lives Matter May Be the Largest Movement in U. S. History," by Buchanan, Bui and Patel. https://www.nytimes.com/interactive/2020/07/03/us/george-floyd-protests-crowd-size.html

9 The three co-founders to the BLM movement in 2017 are Patrisse Kahn-Cullors, Alicia Garza, and Opal Tometi. The three women consider themselves to be Marxists. See a memoir written by Patrisse Khan-Cullors and Asha Bandele with a foreword by Angela Davis entitled *When they call you a terrorist* for an invigorating accounting of personal history that shapes in part the founding of a grass roots (horizontal) movement (2017).

10 Racial (Slavery) Capitalism is a term coined by Cedric Robinson appropriated from other intellectuals who made reference to South Africa's economy under apartheid. What made capitalism racial, he argued was that racisms had already permeated Western society and was expanded in the colonial process of invasion, expropriation, settlement, and racial hierarchy throughout Europe and its colonies including the United States (Robinson, 2000, p. 3). Until recently, US academia maintained a strong division between the analysis of capitalism and slavery but this is no longer the case (Clegg, 2020; Singh, 2017).

11 Jennifer Eberhardt argues throughout her text that Blacks (and people of color) in the US are disproportionately discriminated against when dealing with the police, the criminal justice system, in hiring and receiving promotions, when applying for a loan or mortgage, in stores or restaurants, when voting in elections, and when seeking medical treatment, political and corporate parity, to name a few obvious well know examples (2019).

12 McGowan devotes an entire text on the topic of the psychic cost of the capitalism entitled: *Capitalism and Desire the Psychic Cost of Free Markets* (2016). As a Lacanian academic, he argues that the structures of capitalism mimics and thereby seduces our subjective desires thereby hiding the trauma the system inflicts. Summing up the complexities of capitalism's permeating grip he states: "capitalism protects us-from the encounter with the public, from our gaze, from sacrifice, from the absence of guarantees, from infinitude, from our non-productivity, from love, and even from abundance. But it does enable us to experience the sublime in everyday life" (p. 18).

13 Noted in MLK's text *Testament of Hope the Essential Writings and Speeches of Martin Luther King, Jr.* (1991) from which this quote is obtained: "The black revolution is much more than a struggle for the rights of Negroes. It is forcing America to face all its interrelated flaws—racism, poverty, militarism, and materialism. It is exposing evils that are deeply rooted in the whole structure of our society…and suggests that radical reconstruction of society itself is the real issue to be faced" (p. 313).

14 Žižek, in *Sublime Object of Ideology* (1989) enters into a discussion between Marxist fetishism and that of Lacan. In the capitalist world the place of fetishism shifts from intersubjective relations to relations between things. The crucial social relations are those of production and are no longer transparent. The true relations of domination and servitude (master/slave, police officer/black man) are repressed and disguise themselves during this transition from feudalism (pre-capitalism) to capitalism, thus producing a Marxian symptom (26). In other words, the power dynamics inherent in institutionalized racism in the US is underground, implicit but played out in the commodification (thing making) of black and brown peoples. The constitution, the purveyor of civility is also fetishized into thingness because another dominating, yet invisible discourse dominates the actions of some police officers, their governmental officials that support or influence a militarized interpretation of law and order mandates of protection promised within American Universalism that abject alterity. What is lost in the commodification of the Constitution is that intersubjective relationships. *People become things to be managed and care as a mandate becomes an artifact to be interpreted at the will of the one in power.*

15 Referencing the scholarship of academics whose work focuses on the unique time signatures of another culture opens me to the danger of conflating, denigrating or reifying what is unique about apartheid moment of history. My focus is to advance and particularize what is relevant from the studies of others into the present study.

16 George vigorously outlines his arguments throughout his 2016 text entitled *Trauma and Race A Lacanian Study of African American Racial Identity.* My summarization of his arguments in this paragraph are in part influenced by a live seminar conducted by George and sponsored by the New School for Analytical Psychology on November 7, 2020.

17 George describes the unifying and protective function of communal activities initiated by slaves such as music and religious worship. Not until post-Reconstruction when an emerging black middle class would establish itself could its intelligentsia attain sufficient levels of agency over the discourses to re-signify black history and a politicality to redeploy political force against racialized essentialisms. However, George again makes the claim that that re-signifying discourses (historical correction and political presence) while crucial are not enough.

18 Italian activist Antonio Gramsci identified similar revolutionary temporalities in one of the four elements or schemas (of revolution) regarding various revolts in

Western Europe in response to the French Revolution that that he portrayed thus: "a long submerged process of political and social fragmentation of the restoration…successive small waves of reform rather than by revolutionary explosions,…whereby social struggles find sufficiently elastic frameworks to allow the bourgeoisie to gain power without dramatic upheavals. (Gramsci, 2014, pp. 114–118).

19 See NYT article by Nate Cohn, January 7, 2021: https://www.nytimes.com/2021/01/07/upshot/warnock-ossoff-georgia-victories.html

20 I would be deviating from the thrust of my central thesis if I critique Lacan's 1945 essay directly on the question of ethicality of trans-subjectivity or on the degree to which he begins to refer to concepts in this essay that he later develops more fully. Briefly, Lacan will later develop his conceptualization of the real, the integrative flux of the three registers, *object a*, master signifier and anxiety to which he only alludes in 1945. I reference these later developments somewhat in this chapter and especially in chapter two where I focus entirely on a clinical application of a group process through the lens of this essay.

21 I am not in a position to structurally analyze Render through Lacan's three moments of structural time on many levels. First, Render is not a patient, an intimate friend nor do I have intimate insight into his being not to mention his permission. Most crucially, as a white person, I hold a different subject position whose only intersection to the effects of racialized experience comes to me by listening to his speech in an otherwise shared moment of history. I rely on my own transcription of Render's speech to illustrate aspects of Lacan's three moments of logical time.

22 (Colbert, 2020) When later asked by Stephen Colbert why he had agreed to speak when he clearly didn't want to be there, Render modestly replied that he was a rapper and could not tell anybody what to do. "*I didn't want to get on the podium because I didn't think I had anything to say so I just said what was on my heart, to unite as a worker class.*" YouTube interview: https://www.youtube.com/watch?v=RC8jnN-zp5M

23 In Chapter Two, I conduct a clinical reading of Lacan's 1946 essay where I go into some depth about the structural dynamics of the psychoanalytic subject in relation to a specific group therapy process. In this essay, I follow a similar template, but I do not direct my study into the psychodynamics of Render's subjectivity and only loosely refer to the general subjective processes that Lacan elaborates in his essay. My focus instead is to take aspects of Lacan's three movements of logical time as they apply to the sociopolitical temporal dimensions of a specific catastrophe. I only make loose associations to what Render conveys in his speech in relation to what he actually said in his speech that emerged from a background of structural US racism.

24 American literature, film and cultural critique abound with depictions of the reals of racialized experience. Patrisse Kahn-Cullors (a co-founder of the BLM movement)

describes her first-hand experience of watching police officers violate of her brothers in Los Angeles (Kahn-Cullors & Bandele, 2017). She states: "It's from behind the gate that I watch the police roll up on my brothers and their friends, not one of whom is over the age of 14 and all of whom are doing absolutely nothing but talking. They throw them up on the wall. They make them pull their shirts up. They make them turn out their pockets. They roughly touch my brothers' bodies, even their privates, while behind the gate, I watch, frozen. I cannot cry or scream. I cannot breathe and I cannot hear anything. Later I will be angry with myself: Why didn't I help them? They will not cry or cuss. They will not make loud although empty threats. They will not discuss it with me, who was a witness, or my mother who was not. They will not be outraged. They will not say they do not deserve such treatment. Because by the time they hit puberty, neither will my brothers have expected that things could be another way" (pp. 14–15).

25 The sight of George Floyd's death evokes an outpouring of unconscious fantasies (via the Imaginary register) generated by structural ambiguities of intersubjective engagements of all kinds that are seeded by the initial subject–object relationship. The neonate subject becoming, in Lacan's cannon is from the onset of life embroiled in enigma of the others desire. Desire is always related to what the subject is lacking, and that is predicated by the enigma of the other's lack. What I desire is not my own, but predicated by the other's desire, the big Other's, a desire that exceeds me and thus impossible to comprehend, articulate, or satisfy. I discuss more fully how desire animates the drives and *jouissance* expressions in the previous chapter.

26 There are several sites one may view Render's speech if you were not in Atlanta to hear it live or watch it on CNN. Here is one site: You Tube: https://www.youtube.com/watch?v=Vy9io6VEt58

27 This remark echoes Achille Mbembe's depiction of the difficulties of black South African's to project themselves forward in time because of the crippling repetition of cultural subjugation that contributes to an inability to project themselves into a future of one's own (in Hook, 2015, p. 49; Mbembe, 2013, p. 29; Render, 2020).

28 Mike names local political activists and black city builders within the Atlanta community who built a more racially integrated metropolis. Render stated: "It was people like my grandmother, people like my aunt and uncles who were members of SCLC and the NWACP and in particular Reverend James Orange, Mrs. Alice Johnston, and Reverend Love who we just lost last year."

29 Building on the work of Gilbert Simondon, Bernard Stiegler elaborates this point. "Such a process of internal phase shifting, which is what any dynamic system amounts to, always conditions psychic and collective individuation (Stiegler, 2019, p. 51).

30 I refer to the final lines of Kass Kinkead's poem cited in the header of the introduction that states; "To a future we can fall in love with."

References

Benjamin, W. (1968). *Illuminations Essays and Reflections.* New York: Schocken Books.

Brewster, F. (2019). *Archetypal Grief Slavery's Legacy of Intergenerational Child Loss.* London and New York: Routledge Taylor & Francis Group.

Brooks, R. M. (2016). The international transmission of the catastrophic effects of real world history expressed through the analytic subject. In *Ethics of Evil Psychoanalytic Explorations*, 137–176, Eds. R. Naso & J. Mills. London: Karnac Books.

Buchanan, L., Bui, Q., & Patel, J. K. (July 3, 2020). 'Black lives matter may be the largest movement in U.S. history' retrieved from: https://www.nytimes.com/interactive/2020/07/03/us/george-floyd-protests-crowd-size.html

Butler, J. (2004). *The Psychic Life of Power: Theories of Subjection.* Stanford: Stanford University Press.

Clegg, J. J. (2018). A classical-Marxian model of antebellum slavery. *Cambridge Journal of Economics.* 64, 1, 24.

Clegg, J. J. (2020). A theory of capitalist slavery. *Journal of Historical Sociology.* 33, 1, 74–98.

Cohn, N. (January 7, 2021). *New York Times* retrieved from: https://www.nytimes.com/2021/01/07/upshot/warnock-ossoff-georgia-victories.html

Colbert, S. (June 20, 2020). *YouTube* interview Stephen Colbert with Killer Mike. Late Night with Stephen Colbert retrieved from: https://www.youtube.com/watch?v=RC8jnN-zp5M

Crapanzano, C. (1985). *Waiting: The Whites of South Africa.* Toronto, London, Sydney, New York, Granada: Random House.

Eberhardt, J. (2019). *Biased Uncovering the Hidden Prejudice That Shapes What We See, Think and Do.* New York: Viking.

Fanon, F. (1952). *Black Skin, White Masks.* New York: Grove Press.

George, S. (2016). *Trauma and Race: A Lacanian Study of African American Racial Identity.* Waco, TX: Baylor University Press.

George, S. (2020). A Lacanian study of African American racial identity. Notes from a Seminar sponsored by the New School for Analytical Psychology on November, 7.

Gramsci, A. (2014). *Selections from the Prison Notebooks* (A. Hoare & G. N. Smith, Eds.). New York: International Publishers.

Heidegger, M. (2000). *Being and Time.* New York: Harper One Publishers.

Hook, D. (2012). *A Critical Psychology of the Postcolonial: The Mind of Apartheid.* London and New York: Psychology Press Taylor & Francis Group.

Hook, D. (2013). *(Post) Apartheid Conditions Psychoanalysis and Social Formation*. New York: Palgrave Macmillan.

Hook, D. (2015). Infinite delay: On (post) apartheid temporality. In *Psychosocial Imaginaries Perspectives on Temporality, Subjectivities and Activism*, Ed. S. Frosh. New York: Palgrave Macmillan.

Hook, D. (2018). *Six Moments in Lacan*. London and New York: Routledge.

Kahn-Cullors, P., & Bandele, A. (2017). *When They Call You a Terrorist*. New York: St. Martin's Press.

King, M. L. (1991). *A Testament of Hope: The Essential Writings and Speeches Martin Luther King, Jr*. New York: HarperOne.

Kristeva, J. (1982). *Powers of Horror: An Essay on Abjection*. New York: Columbia University Press.

Lacan, J. (1991). *The Seminar of Jacques Lacan, Book II: The Ego in Freud's Theory and in the Technique of Psychoanalysis* (J. A. Miller, Ed.). New York and London: W. W. Norton.

Lacan, J. (1993). *Seminar of Jacques Lacan: The Psychoses*. New York and London: W.W. Norton.

Lacan, J. (1999). *The Seminar of Jacques Lacan: On Feminine Sexuality, the Limits of Love and Knowledge (Encore Edition) (Vol. Book XX)* (J. A. Miller, Ed.). New York and London: W.W. Norton.

Lacan, J. (2006). *Ecrits: The First Completed Edition in English*. New York and London: W. W. Norton.

Lacan, J. (2014). *Anxiety: The Seminar of Jacques Lacan, Book X* (J. A. Miller, Ed.). Cambridge: Polity Press.

Mbembe, A. (2013). Consumed by our lust for lost segregation. *The Mail & Guardian* retrieved from: https://mg.co.za/article/2013-03-28-00-consumed-by-our-lust-for-lost-segregation/. Accessed 9/10/21.

McGowan, T. (2016). *Capitalism and Desire*. New York: Columbia University Press.

Mouffe, C. (1993). *The Return of the Political*. London: Verso.

Render, S. M. (2020). 'Killer Mike's emotional speech at Atlanta Mayor's press conference' retrieved from: https://www.youtube.com/watch?v=RC8jnN-zp5M

Robinson, C. R. (2000). *Black Marxism: The Making of the Black Radical Tradition*. Chapel Hill and London: University of North Carolina Press.

Robinson, C. R. (2016). *The Terms of Order: Political Science and the Myth of Leadership*. Chapel Hill and London: University of North Carolina Press.

Simondon, G. (1992). The genesis of the individual. In *Incorporations*, Eds. J. Crary & S. Kwinter. New York: Zone.

Singh, N. P. (2005). *Black Is a Country: Race and the Unfinished Struggle for Democracy*. Cambridge, MA, and London: Harvard University Press.

Singh, N. P. (2017). *Race and America's Long War*. Oakland, CA: University of California Press.

Singh, N. P., Burc, R., & Souvlis, G. (July 3, 2020). 'Race and America's long war: An interview with Nikhal Pal Singh' retrieved from: https://salvage.zone/articles/race-and-americas-long-war-an-interview-with-nikhil-pal-singh/

Stavrakakis, Y. (1999). *Lacan and the Political*. London: Routledge.

Stiegler, R. (2019). *The Age of Disruption Technology and Madness in Computational Capitalism*. Malden, MA: Polity Press.

Webster, J. (2018). *Conversion Disorder: Listening to the Body in Psychoanalysis*. New York: Columbia University Press.

Wolff, R. (2012). *Democracy at Work: A Cure for Capitalism*. Chicago, IL: Haymarker Books.

Žižek, S. (1989). *The Sublime Object of Ideology*. London and New York: Verso.

Žižek, S. (1994). The spectre of ideology. In *Mapping Ideology*. London and New York: Verso.

Žižek, S. (2006). *The Parallax View*. Cambridge, MA: MIT Press.

Žižek, S. (2008). *The Sublime Object of Ideology*. London and New York: Verso.

Žižek, S. (2013). *Demanding the Impossible*. Cambridge, MA: Polity Press.

Index

105, 120, 123, 126, 128n9, 131n21, 134–63; dimension of significance 113–15, 134
Trump, D. 8, 125, 138

US (post) slavery racism: political temporality of 137–40; socio/political temporality of 140–7; structural racism 147–54; trans-subjective agency 134–63
Valéry, P. 68n1

Webster, J.: "Conversion Disorder: The Body as Revolt" 159n4
white superiority, fantasy construction of 13
Winnicott, W. 22, 109
"working through" 79, 99

Žižek, S. 25, 26, 30–1n19, 39, 43–6, 51, 54, 56, 69n13, 69n14, 71n22; political theory 40–1; *Sublime Object of Ideology* 161n14

For Product Safety Concerns and Information please contact our EU
representative GPSR@taylorandfrancis.com
Taylor & Francis Verlag GmbH, Kaufingerstraße 24, 80331 München, Germany